THE
RUSSIAN
KREMLIN

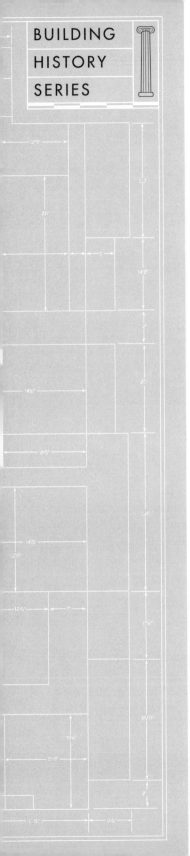

BUILDING
HISTORY
SERIES

THE RUSSIAN KREMLIN

by Meg Greene

Lucent Books, Inc., San Diego, California

Library of Congress Cataloging-in-Publication Data

Greene, Meg.
  The Russian Kremlin / by Meg Greene.
    p.   cm. — (Building history series)
  Includes bibliographical references and index.
  ISBN 1-56006-840-X (hardback : alk. paper)
  1. Kremlin (Moscow, Russia)—Juvenile literature. 2.
Architecture—Russia (Federation)—Moscow—Juvenile literature.
3. Red Square (Moscow, Russia)—Juvenile literature. [1. Kremlin
(Moscow, Russia) 2. Architecture—Russia (Federation)—Moscow.
3. Red Square (Moscow, Russia)] I. Title.   II. Series.
  NA4415.R92 M62   2001
  720'.947'31—dc21   00-012111

Printed in the U.S.A.

CONTENTS

FOREWORD

Throughout history, as civilizations have evolved and prospered, each has produced unique buildings and architectural styles. Combining the need for both utility and artistic expression, a society's buildings, particularly its large-scale public structures, often reflect the individual character traits that distinguish it from other societies. In a very real sense, then, buildings express a society's values and unique characteristics in tangible form. As scholar Anita Abramovitz comments in her book *People and Spaces*, "Our ways of living and thinking—our habits, needs, fear of enemies, aspirations, materialistic concerns, and religious beliefs—have influenced the kinds of spaces that we build and that later surround and include us."

That specific types and styles of structures constitute an outward expression of the spirit of an individual people or era can be seen in the diverse ways that various societies have built palaces, fortresses, tombs, churches, government buildings, sports arenas, public works, and other such monuments. The ancient Greeks, for instance, were a supremely rational people who originated Western philosophy and science, including the atomic theory and the realization that the earth is a sphere. Their public buildings, epitomized by Athens's magnificent Parthenon temple, were equally rational, emphasizing order, harmony, reason, and above all, restraint.

By contrast, the Romans, who conquered and absorbed the Greek lands, were a highly practical people preoccupied with acquiring and wielding power over others. The Romans greatly admired and readily copied elements of Greek architecture, but modified and adapted them to their own needs. "Roman genius was called into action by the enormous practical needs of a world empire," wrote historian Edith Hamilton. "Rome met them magnificently. Buildings tremendous, indomitable, amphitheaters where eighty thousand could watch a spectacle, baths where three thousand could bathe at the same time."

In medieval Europe, God heavily influenced and motivated the people, and religion permeated all aspects of society, molding people's worldviews and guiding their everyday actions. That spiritual mindset is reflected in the most important medieval structure—the Gothic cathedral—which, in a sense, was a model of heavenly cities. As scholar Anne Fremantle so elegantly phrases it, the cathedrals were "harmonious elevations of stone and glass reaching up to heaven to seek and receive the light [of God]."

Our more secular modern age, in contrast, is driven by the realities of a global economy, advanced technology, and mass communications. Responding to the needs of international trade and the growth of cities housing millions of people, today's builders construct engineering marvels, among them towering skyscrapers of steel and glass, mammoth marine canals, and huge and elaborate rapid transit systems, all of which would have left their ancestors, even the Romans, awestruck.

In examining some of humanity's greatest edifices, Lucent Books' Building History series recognizes this close relationship between a society's historical character and its buildings. Each volume in the series begins with a historical sketch of the people who erected the edifice, exploring their major achievements as well as the beliefs, customs, and societal needs that dictated the variety, functions, and styles of their buildings. A detailed explanation of how the selected structure was conceived, designed, and built, to the extent that this information is known, makes up the majority of the volume.

Each volume in the Lucent Building History series also includes several special features that are useful tools for additional research. A chronology of important dates gives students an overview, at a glance, of the evolution and use of the structure described. Sidebars create a broader context by adding further details on some of the architects, engineers, and construction tools, materials, and methods that made each structure a reality, as well as the social, political, and/or religious leaders and movements that inspired its creation. Useful maps help the reader locate the nations, cities, streets, and individual structures mentioned in the text; and numerous diagrams and pictures illustrate tools and devices that bring to life various stages of construction. Finally, each volume contains two bibliographies, one for student research, the other listing works the author consulted in compiling the book.

Taken as a whole, these volumes, covering diverse ancient and modern structures, constitute not only a valuable research tool, but also a tribute to the human spirit, a fascinating exploration of the dreams, skills, ingenuity, and dogged determination of the great peoples who shaped history.

IMPORTANT DATES IN THE BUILDING OF THE RUSSIAN KREMLIN

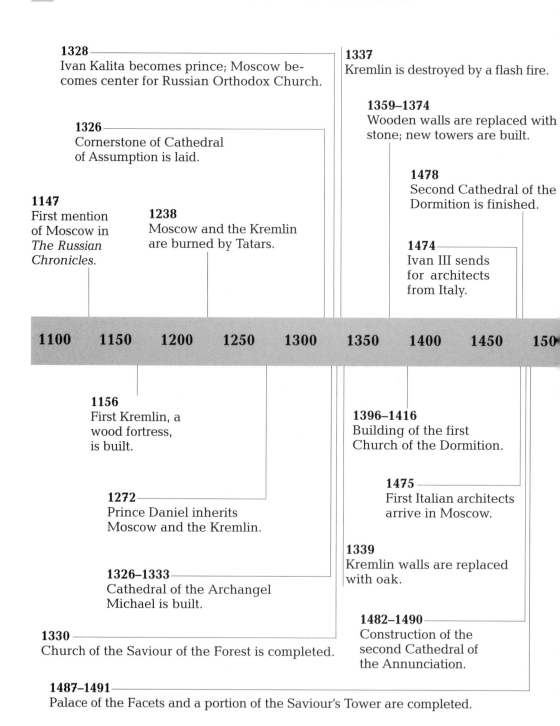

1328
Ivan Kalita becomes prince; Moscow becomes center for Russian Orthodox Church.

1337
Kremlin is destroyed by a flash fire.

1359–1374
Wooden walls are replaced with stone; new towers are built.

1326
Cornerstone of Cathedral of Assumption is laid.

1478
Second Cathedral of the Dormition is finished.

1147
First mention of Moscow in *The Russian Chronicles.*

1238
Moscow and the Kremlin are burned by Tatars.

1474
Ivan III sends for architects from Italy.

| 1100 | 1150 | 1200 | 1250 | 1300 | 1350 | 1400 | 1450 | 150 |

1156
First Kremlin, a wood fortress, is built.

1396–1416
Building of the first Church of the Dormition.

1475
First Italian architects arrive in Moscow.

1272
Prince Daniel inherits Moscow and the Kremlin.

1339
Kremlin walls are replaced with oak.

1326–1333
Cathedral of the Archangel Michael is built.

1330
Church of the Saviour of the Forest is completed.

1482–1490
Construction of the second Cathedral of the Annunciation.

1487–1491
Palace of the Facets and a portion of the Saviour's Tower are completed.

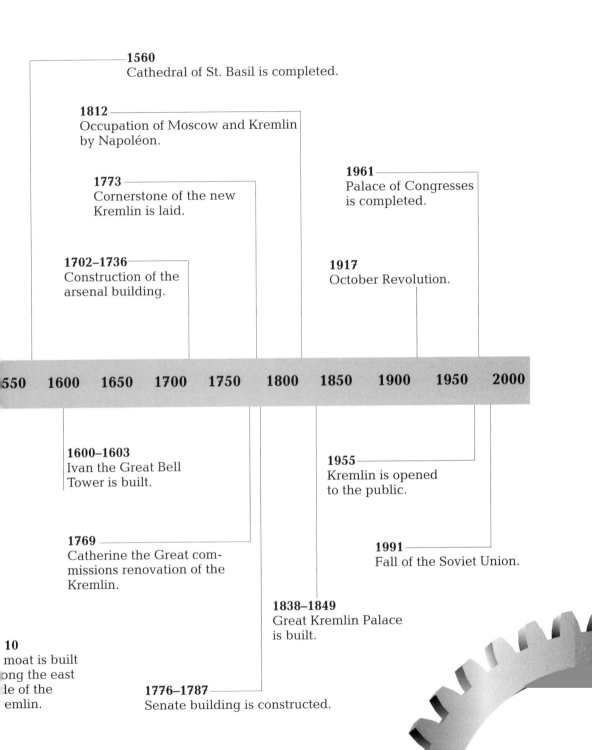

1560
Cathedral of St. Basil is completed.

1812
Occupation of Moscow and Kremlin
by Napoléon.

1961
Palace of Congresses
is completed.

1773
Cornerstone of the new
Kremlin is laid.

1702–1736
Construction of the
arsenal building.

1917
October Revolution.

550   1600   1650   1700   1750   1800   1850   1900   1950   2000

1600–1603
Ivan the Great Bell
Tower is built.

1955
Kremlin is opened
to the public.

1769
Catherine the Great com-
missions renovation of the
Kremlin.

1991
Fall of the Soviet Union.

1838–1849
Great Kremlin Palace
is built.

10
moat is built
ong the east
le of the
emlin.

1776–1787
Senate building is constructed.

INTRODUCTION

"Those who have seen it at the first flush of dawn, or have watched its colors fade with the setting sun, will long remember its moving beauty."[1] So remarked a noted art historian describing the Kremlin. For him, as for many others, the sight of the Kremlin is unforgettable.

It was not always that way, however. More than eight hundred years ago the Moscow Kremlin was just one of many small walled communities dotting the Russian landscape. These central fortresses, usually located at strategic points along a waterway, were often separated from the city proper by a wooden, and later a stone or brick, wall. Towers, battlements (a wall built with indented openings along the top of a tower), and a moat offered protection against invaders and ensured the safety of the inhabitants.

The word *kremlin*, or *Kreml*, first appeared in 1331 in an account of a fire that ravaged Moscow. The term described a fortress. For unknown reasons, the term disappeared from Russian documents for nearly two centuries. In 1589, however, *kremlin* resurfaced in connection with Moscow. It has been in use ever since to describe one of the most unusual and fascinating places in the world.

The Moscow Kremlin was not the first, or even the finest, of these walled towns. In fact, during its early years few people knew of the tiny and remote settlement. The cities of Novogorod, Suzdal', and Pskov all boasted kremlins that were much older, larger, and more elaborate than the one built in Moscow. In the end, though, it was the Moscow Kremlin that survived and emerged as one of the most architecturally splendid complexes in the world.

Throughout its history, the Kremlin has housed a staggering array of buildings. These have included magnificent churches and cathedrals, grand palaces, and the majestic homes of the boyars, the high-ranking Russian nobility. The Kremlin today is home to a historical museum, a theater, and a modern office building. It has been the dwelling place of Russian royalty, the center of both the Russian and Soviet empires, and the heart of the Russian Orthodox Church. It is the place where Russia's most valuable artistic and historical treasures are found. The history of the Kremlin, then is also the history of Moscow and, in many ways, the history of Russia.

The Kremlin's structures provide an excellent example of medieval fortifications.

AN ARCHITECTURAL WONDER

The Kremlin is one of the most architecturally significant structures in the world. With its watchtowers, battlements, ramparts, and multicolored towers, the Kremlin presents an impressive example of medieval fortifications. Located within its walls are palaces made of beautiful marble and white stone and decorated with multicolored tiles and shiny metal surfaces. There are also the cathedrals, one with dazzling colored onion-shaped domes; another covered with polychrome, or multicolored, walls; and still others with cupolas blanketed in gold and silver and roofs of finely crafted enameled inlays. The Kremlin stands as a magnificent collection of buildings that blends the past and the present, the East and the West.

Located almost directly in the center of Moscow, the Kremlin is an irregularly shaped pentagon, measuring approximately 1.5 miles at its perimeter and enclosing almost 65 acres. It stands atop a hill almost 125 feet above the Moskva and Neglinnaya Rivers, which border it to the south. To the east is the famous Red Square, a site that has played an important role in the

Located in the center of Moscow, the Kremlin is shaped like an irregular pentagon.

history of the Kremlin. To the west lies Alexander Park. Once surrounded by heavy woods, the Kremlin today is flanked by the highways and streets of Moscow.

Instead of straight, lengthy walls, which were the most common form of fort construction, the walls of the Kremlin were built in straight, short lines. These lines were then broken at intervals by the placement of a wall piece that zigzagged slightly. This was done for the purposes of defense, making it difficult for enemies to ascend the walls. Additionally, on the south side the wall curves somewhat to follow the bend of the Moskva River. Even with its unusual construction, and despite being rebuilt several times during its history, the Kremlin has, for the most part, retained its original shape. Yet with each reconstruction, the fortress gradually expanded to make room for the new buildings periodically added to the compound.

AN ABLE DEFENDER

From the outset the Kremlin was designed to withstand heavy attacks. Each new design modification shows careful thought and attention to the prevailing theories of military defense, such as accommodating the invention of gunpowder in the eleventh century and the use of firearms by the fourteenth.

One of the components that underwent continuous modification were the Kremlin walls, which were constructed first of wood, then stone, then solid brick, and which were anywhere from twelve to sixteen feet thick. Yet even with all of the rebuilding, the walls of the modern Kremlin look much as they did more than a century ago. They are constructed of crenellated (notched at the top of the wall) red brick, and if stretched out, they would span a distance of 2,444 yards, roughly the length of twenty football fields.

Twenty towers, nineteen of them with steeples, mark various points along the walls. Located at each corner are circular towers. There are five gate, or entrance, towers. Eleven observation towers survey the area outside the Kremlin, and barbicans, or watchtowers, located above the entrance gates once guarded against intruders. The entrance towers also enjoyed additional protection with the construction of drawbridges that could be raised or lowered as needed.

WITNESS TO HISTORY

For more than eight hundred years the majestic domes, elaborate towers, and massive walls of the Kremlin have dominated Moscow's skyline. From its rough beginnings in 1156 as a crude wooden fortress, the Kremlin has stood as a silent sentinel to the

A UNIQUE DESIGN

Unlike the exacting and symmetrical rectangles and octagons that composed western European fortifications, the architects of the Kremlin built the fort to blend in with the surrounding terrain. The walls follow the contours, or shapes, of the land. The Kremlin walls travel up and down small hills, adding another unique dimension to its overall design. Because of this, the wall height and thickness vary, ranging anywhere from sixteen to sixty-two feet high and eleven to twenty-one feet thick. This unusual design is another feature that makes the Kremlin so distinct.

Although the Kremlin's crenellated walls have undergone many modifications over the years, they still look much as they did more than a century ago.

city's triumphs, tribulations, and tragedies. It was both a victor over, and the victim of, the many invaders who swept into Moscow. With the formation of the Muscovite empire in the thirteenth century, the Kremlin evolved into the political, religious, and cultural center not only for the city but also, in time, for all of Russia. A frontier fortress in which city residents sought safety, the Kremlin also became the final resting place of czars and czarinas, the kings and queens of Russia.

Then, in the early twentieth century, the Kremlin, showing signs of age and the scars of battle, emerged as the center of a new and radical government, the Communist Union of Soviet Socialist Republics (USSR). For more than seventy years the fortress became virtually synonymous with Communism. But with the collapse of the Soviet Union in 1991, the Kremlin once again adapted itself to the changes taking place in Russian history. No longer the residence of czars or Soviet premiers, it is now home to Russian presidents.

A CITADEL OF WOOD

Shrouded in myth and mystery, the origins of the Kremlin remain obscure. To compensate, the Russian people have invented a number of stories to illuminate the past. For generations, these legendary tales explained different facets of Moscow and the Kremlin. One common element in most of these tales is a Russian family by the name of Kuchka.

THE SIGN OF THE DOUBLE EAGLE

The earliest history of the Kremlin and Moscow begins with the story of Stephen Kuchka, the son of a powerful nobleman. Legend has it that one day while hunting near the Moskva River, Kuchka came upon a huge, fierce boar. Frightened, Kuchka turned to run. Suddenly a large eagle with immense wings, giant claws, and two heads swooped down from the sky. The bird scooped up the boar and flew to the nearby hill overlooking the Moskva River. Kuchka followed the flight of the bird. When he reached the crest of the hill and looked down, he saw the remains of the boar below. He decided to build a small wooden hut on the spot near the river to use as a hunting lodge. Surrounding it, he had a trench dug and disguised with leafy branches. Near this spot was built the first Kremlin, and the two-headed eagle would become the national symbol of Russia and its rulers.

Another legend involving the Kuchka family is bloodier. In the late twelfth century, Prince Daniel of Suzdal', a kingdom located in north-central Russia, reached the Moskva River. According to the legend, Prince Daniel came upon the "beautiful hamlets [towns] of the goodly *boyar* [a high-ranking nobleman] by the name of Stephen Ivanovich Kuchka."[2] Kuchka was the proud father of two sons, who everyone agreed were the most handsome boys in all of Russia. They so captivated Prince Daniel that he invited them to serve at his royal court.

The two Kuchka boys quickly adapted to their new life, and soon they held important positions in the court. Unfortunately, both fell under the spell of the prince's wife, Ulita, who many

15

Russia's national symbol, the two-headed eagle, was inspired by the legend of Stephen Kuchka's founding a building site for the Kremlin.

believed to be possessed by the devil. Both brothers began love affairs with her. Fearing that Prince Daniel would discover these forbidden relationships, the three plotted to murder him. When the prince went off on a hunting trip, the brothers followed and speared him to death. After cutting off his head, they hid the prince's body in a secluded peasant's hut. The brothers returned to Ulita and resumed their affairs with her.

Upon hearing of Daniel's death, his brother, Prince Andrei of Vladimir, gathered an army and marched to Suzdal'. When he arrived, he arrested Ulita and then executed her for his brother's murder. Fearing the worst, the Kuchka brothers fled to their father's estate. Andrei followed and killed both boys and their father.

After avenging his brother's death, Andrei surveyed the Kuchka lands. The legend, further states, that God told him to build a great city on the site of one of the villages near the Moskva River. A devout man, the prince obeyed, and soon the town of Moscow and the Kremlin were born.

Although both stories are legends, they contain some factual elements. There did exist a noble family by the name of Kuchka who lived near the present site of Moscow; as late as the seventeenth century, the Moskva River was also known as "Moscow, the Kuchka River." But beyond that, the history of the Kuchkas, like the beginnings of Moscow and the Kremlin, seem destined always to remain something of a mystery.

AN OBSCURE TOWN

The first official historical reference to the Moscow Kremlin appears in *The Russian Chronicles*, an early history of Russia. The author of *The Russian Chronicles* recorded that in 1147 Yury Dolgoruky, prince of Suzdal', on his way home from a military campaign, invited Prince Sviatoslav of Novhorod-Sivers'kyy to Moscow for a great banquet. "Come to me Brother, to Moscow,"[3] Dolgoruky said. Based on this information, historians have speculated that Dolgoruky had built some sort of blockhouse and large warehouse that could accommodate supplies and visitors.

Historians know with greater certainty that in 1156 Dolgoruky laid out the parameters of the city of Moscow by building a wall made of pine logs, stones, and bricks around the building used for the banquet with Prince Sviatoslav. They think that this small fortress, located in the western corner of the modern Kremlin, was approximately one-third the size of the Kremlin that exists today. This little Kremlin also had a number of small wooden towers and gates.

Early in the thirteenth century a ruthless prince named Batu Khan of Mongolia invaded the tiny settlement and burned it and the surrounding area to the ground. All that remained of the town and the fortress were heaps of smoldering ashes. Batu Khan's invasion was the first in a brutal series of raids from the east and south that plagued Moscow well into the fourteenth century and beyond.

Undaunted, the people of Moscow rebuilt their city and their fort. By this time Moscow was under the leadership of Prince Yaroslav, a distant relative of Yury Dolgoruky. Sometime during

A CONSTANT THREAT

Occurring almost daily, fires were a constant danger to Moscow and the Kremlin. One of the problems was that many of the early homes had fireplaces or stoves but no chimneys, increasing the threat of fire. Because of this ongoing hazard, wood merchants, who were stationed near the main gate to the city, sold precut replacement logs. In this way, a house that burned down in the morning would be standing once more by the following day.

the reconstruction, however, Yaroslav died. His son, Mikhail, inherited his father's position as well as the great task of rebuilding Moscow and the Kremlin. An eyewitness account dated from around 1250 describes the rebuilding process:

> The prince [Mikhail] was energetic and courageous in his work. He worked with all his might to rebuild his beloved Kremlin. . . . He supervised the work of reconstruction in person, occasionally taking pick or axe and working alongside the laborers or helping the carpenters. . . . To those who did good work the prince would distribute bonuses from his own pocket.[4]

The rebuilding process took ten years to complete. A contemporary account, written at the time of Mikhail's death in 1248, stated that the Kremlin boasted "six gates in the place of four, five churches instead of two, a new palace with many-colored mica [a metalloid material] windows and buildings for the *druzhina* [soldiers and advisers to the prince] and the boyars."[5] The fort and its new structures still faced the continual threat of destruction, though, as almost all of the new additions were made of wood and badly fired Russian bricks, which were not known for their strength.

A CITY OF WOOD

During this period, because of the scarcity of stone, wood was used as the primary building material. However, there were certain limitations in building with wood. The height and size of buildings, for instance, were somewhat limited. Because of this, the palaces and churches of early Russia tended to be much smaller than the great stone castles and cathedrals found in western Europe and England.

The materials available for construction also more or less dictated the Russian architectural style. Building with wood evolved into a highly sophisticated form of architecture that was unique in appearance and decoration. Wood was used for almost every type of building construction, from great churches to royal residences to simple peasant huts. The structures in the Kremlin were no exception.

Building with wood almost always meant using pine or oak. After drying the wood, the building process began. Russian wood construction was noted for its use of "block work," a technique in which round pine logs were laid in vertical rows and interlocked at the building's corners. Each log was slightly hollowed out near the bottom to fit over the top of the log beneath it. Any spaces were then filled in with moss or oakum to keep out the cold and dampness.

To build these solid wooden walls, all the builder needed was an axe. Saws and nails were unnecessary because of the interlocking design. The building's outside walls were left as they were, but the inside walls were axe-hewen into a smooth surface. Once the walls were in place, the roof was added. Elaborately painted wood carvings, ornate windows and doors, and beautifully carved wooden chimneys provided the final touches to the finished building.

Since they had to hold up under heavy winter snows, roofs on Russian buildings were often gabled. A gabled roof is one in which the two roof sides come to a sharp point and form a triangular space between them. At each open end, the Russians enclosed the space with logs of successively shorter lengths. Sometimes a builder might choose to curve or flare out the wall at the roof's eaves (the place where the roof meets the wall). This technique

Early Russian buildings, such as this church, were constructed from wood and had gabled roofs to protect them from winter snows.

provided a kind of projecting shelf and also allowed builders a little creativity in choosing how they shaped the profile of the roof.

Almost always on one roof end, located near the top of the wall, was some type of elaborate wood carving, usually the head of a fantastic bird, goat, deer, or horse. The other end of the building would have the animal's tail in the same spot. This type of decoration was found on houses only and was never employed on barns, churches, or public buildings.

The residences of the Kremlin princes most likely were based on the *izba*, or cottage. The house was basically a chamber or series of chambers heated by fireplaces. To protect the building's residents from the Russian cold and dampness, door and window openings were few. Quite often these royal homes were at least two stories high. Living quarters for the family were reserved for the top floors, and the servants, livestock, and supplies were maintained on the bottom level.

One of the greatest characteristics of Russian architecture is the use of color for decoration of these homes and other buildings. Windows, in particular, were the object of rich decoration. Elaborate and brightly painted carvings often surrounded the window opening. Carved wooden chimneys were also common. Often beginning as slender rectangular forms, they were usually capped with whimsical tops in the shape of the house roof line and with decorated carvings.

Russian windows were the objects of rich decoration.

RUSSIAN CHURCH ARCHITECTURE

The earliest Russian churches, like most other Russian buildings, were made of wood. Many churches showed the early influences of the Byzantine architectural style, which used domes, round arches, and decorative carved columns. But the style was adapted by Russian builders to suit the climate and temperament of their homeland, namely modifying it to use the native wood of Russia rather than stone. Another modification can be seen in the construction of church roofs. Builders cut shingles out of very thin wooden pieces and then shaped their ends like a cross. In the right light, the roofs glimmered and shone as if made of silver.

Topping the steeples of Kremlin churches, the onion dome has become a trademark of Russian architecture.

Among the most distinctive aspects of the Kremlin churches, however, are the onion-shaped domes that top their steeples. Early church domes tended to be more round, following the lines of Byzantine church models. But by the thirteenth century more and more Russian churches were built with what became a trademark architectural element, the onion dome, so-called because of its resemblance to an onion.

Historians have suggested many reasons for this design. Some say that it was adopted for practical purposes. The onion shape made the dome better suited to repel the heavy snows that are a part of the Russian winter. Others believe that the domes acquired their shape for religious reasons: to catch the prayers of the faithful and send them on their way to heaven. Another explanation is that the domes took the form of soldiers' helmets, as Russian churches were symbolic "soldiers," the last

BYZANTINE ARCHITECTURE

The architecture of the Byzantine, or eastern Roman, Empire dates back to the fourth century. The style was noted for its large domes, supported by a set of curved walls resting between the dome and the supporting masonry structure underneath; round arches; and elaborately decorated and carved columns. The style was also famous for its rich use of color and decorative ornament. Byzantine architecture was especially popular in Greece, and it later spread to other parts of Europe and Russia. For Russian builders, the Byzantine style's use of color and decoration was especially appealing and fit well within their own decorative designs. The Byzantine style influenced Russian architecture for well over a century. Even today one can still see wonderful examples of it at the Kremlin, especially in the magnificent Cathedral of St. Basil, built in the sixteenth century by Ivan IV.

The Sveti Leo in Vodoca, an eleventh-century example of Byzantine architecture, features a round dome, round arches, and ornate columns.

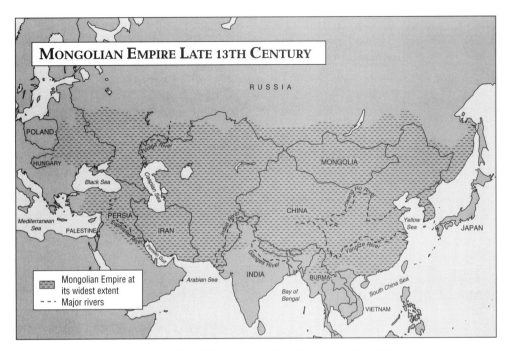

Mongolian Empire Late 13th Century

RUSSIA

POLAND

HUNGARY

Black Sea

Volga River

Caspian Sea

MONGOLIA

Mediterranean Sea

PERSIA

PALESTINE

Euphrates River

Persian Gulf

IRAN

Indus River

Huang Ho River

CHINA

Yellow Sea

JAPAN

Ganges River

Yangtze River

Arabian Sea

INDIA

BURMA

South China Sea

Bay of Bengal

VIETNAM

Mongolian Empire at its widest extent

- - - Major rivers

line of defense to protect the West from the East and the Christian faith from the Islam of the dreaded Tatars and Turks. Whatever the reason, for centuries, the Kremlin's church domes remained one of the most distinctive and recognized features of Russian churches.

A Capital Is Born

The Tatars, also known as the Mongols, originated in the kingdom of Mongolia, located to the south of Russia. Over the course of the next 226 years, between 1236 and 1462, the Tatars invaded Russia forty-eight times and nearly conquered the entire country. By the time the Tatar domination was complete, their empire stretched from modern China to what is now Hungary. The Adriatic coast lay to the north and the Chinese border to the south. Within this great empire, 1 million Tatars ruled 100 million Russians for the next 250 years.

In the midst of this turmoil, control of Moscow and the Kremlin passed to a young prince named Daniel Aleksandrovich, who had received the town and surrounding villages as an inheritance from his father, Aleksander Nevsky, in 1263. Under Daniel's rule, Moscow grew and, in time, became the capital of his kingdom. Daniel controlled the strategically important mouth of the Moskva

River, making the city a key commercial and military center. What made this situation all the more remarkable was that the sum total of Prince Daniel's holdings amounted to little more than five hundred square miles.

During Daniel's reign the Kremlin also began to take on a more substantial shape. By this time the fortress was triangular, with the city of Moscow surrounding it. As Moscow grew, the walls on the side of the Kremlin facing the river were simply extended; a new wall was built around the existing one. The appearance of these concentric walls was similar to the growth rings of a tree. Daniel also built new churches, new palaces, and enlarged the *Terem*, or royal residence. Thus, from its humble beginnings as a small wooden fort, the Kremlin now stood poised and ready to enter the next phase of its and Russia's history.

From Wood
to Stone

By the time of Daniel Aleksandrovich's death in 1303, Moscow and the Kremlin were firmly established as permanent settlements. Daniel's grandson Prince Ivan Danilovich, became Ivan I, but many people referred to him by his nickname, Kalita ("Moneybags"), because of the great money bag he kept strapped to his belt instead of a sword. During these years the Kremlin continued to undergo a great deal of new construction as Kalita set out not only to make it a showplace but also to exhibit Moscow as the new cultural and political center of Russia.

Kalita also set out to enlarge his kingdom. As he acquired more land, either through purchase or confiscation for nonpayment of taxes, the principality of Moscow grew; by the mid–fourteenth century, it was the unofficial capital of Russia. The highest-ranking princes and nobility lived there, and all Kalita had to do was obtain official recognition from the Tatars that Moscow was the nation's capital. In an effort to accomplish this task, Kalita set out to enhance the prestige of Moscow and to continue to attract royalty, nobility, and clergy. Thus, he embarked on a massive building campaign at the Kremlin. He erected a palace of white stone in addition to stone homes for the families of the Russian nobility who chose Moscow as their place of residence.

Kalita's insistence on the use of stone rather than wood was an important innovation. Novgorod, Pskov, and Tver'—cities that rivaled Moscow—all had at least one stone building. If Moscow were going to compete with them, Kalita knew it also would have to have structures built of stone; only in that way could he call attention to the Kremlin and boost the reputation of Moscow as both a military stronghold and a beautiful city. Building with stone, however, presented several problems, not least among them was that there were no local stonemasons in the area. To have his buildings constructed, Kalita brought in stonemasons to carry out the job.

A DRAMATIC TRANSFORMATION

Another important event to take place during Kalita's reign was the transformation of the Kremlin and Moscow into the religious center of the country. This was not the first time that the Russian Orthodox Church had been forced to move to another city. Originally the religious center of Russia was Kiev, a large city to the southwest of Moscow. In 1299, however, because of the repeated threat of Tatar invasions, the metropolitan, the highest-ranking bishop of the Russian Orthodox Church, abandoned Kiev for Vladimir, a city just to the east of Moscow. However, problems arose there as city officials and church authorities entered into a series of disagreements. Finally, in 1328, weary of the dispute, the metropolitan moved the church to Moscow and the Kremlin. With Moscow officials doing their best to accommodate the church, it appeared as if the church had at last found a permanent home.

In time, many Russians came to believe that the choice of Moscow was divinely ordained. According to one legend, the metropolitan actually died in the arms of Kalita after uttering the following words: "My son . . . shouldst build the Church of the Holy Mother, and shouldst lay me to rest in thy city [Moscow], then of a surety will thou be glorified above all other princes in the land . . . and this city will itself be glorified above other Russian towns."[6]

Whether or not this legend is fact, it is clear that Kalita did greatly desire the presence of the church to make Moscow a prestigious as well as holy city. Thus, he ordered a number of church buildings constructed between 1326 and 1333. These included the court of the metropolitan; a church administration building; and three masonry, or stone, churches, the very first ever built in the Kremlin.

FIRE!

Most of the Kremlin, though, was still made of wood and was thus vulnerable to fire. Twice during Kalita's reign, once in 1331 and again in 1337, fire destroyed large portions of the Kremlin. What the fire did not consume, workmen then tore down, and in its place Kalita built walls made with heavy oak timbers, fifty feet long and twenty-eight inches thick. The appearance of the fortress led Moscow to become known not as "the stone city," but rather as "the *grad dubovyi*," or "the oak city." Unfortunately, Kalita did not long enjoy the fruits of his labor; he died in 1340, just one year after completing the rebuilding project.

THE RUSSIAN ORTHODOX CHURCH

The emergence of the Russian Orthodox Church coincides with the rising political stature of Moscow during the fifteenth century. After Constantinople—the capital of the Byzantine Empire—fell to the Muslim Turks in 1453, the czar proclaimed himself as the protector of Orthodox Christianity and declared the Russian Orthodox Church the true successor to the first Orthodox Church that had originated in Byzantium. Throughout its history, this Church has stood as a great source of strength, unity, and faith for the Russian people.

A sixteenth-century Romanian fresco depicts the Muslim Turks seizing Constantinople in 1453.

For the next decade, the people of Moscow battled other disasters. The Black Plague, a terrible and deadly disease, caused numerous deaths, including that of Prince Simeon the Proud, Kalita's successor. Then, in 1349, another great fire swept through the Kremlin. The city recovered much more quickly than it had in the past, though—partly because, as the political and cultural center of the country, Moscow could command more money to finance rebuilding efforts.

GOING TO CHURCH

Russian churches are all very similar in the way they are laid out. Generally square, the churches have a wide central space. A dome is located directly above this space, symbolizing the dome of heaven. Unlike Western churches, Russian Orthodox churches have no pews, chairs, or benches because the faithful believe it is disrespectful to sit in the presence of God. As a result, worshipers stand, no matter how long the service lasts. There is, though, an informality about the Orthodox service; people can come and go as they please, worshiping in their own way. These practices, traditions lasting more than one thousand years, remain a staple of the Russian Orthodox faith.

Worshipers stand through a Russian Orthodox church service at the Kremlin's Cathedral of the Assumption.

IVAN II

Kalita's grandson, Prince Dmitry Ivanovich (also known as Dmitry Donskoi), ascended the throne in 1359. To protect the Kremlin from the still-present threat of invasion, Dmitry ordered the strengthening of the Kremlin walls. The existing wooden walls were torn down, and in 1367 a foundation was laid for the Kremlin's new stone walls to be made of white sandstone, which was specially imported from Miachkov, located fifteen miles from Moscow.

The new walls were made by constructing a revetment, or stone covering, on either side of the existing oak walls. The revetments were then filled with rubble and stones of different shapes and sizes. These new stone fortifications were the first of their kind in this region of Russia. Muscovites noted with pride that not even the wealthier city of Tver' had such a stone wall.

To further strengthen Moscow's defenses, Dmitry rebuilt the Kremlin's battlements. He fortified the new towers with heavy wooden shields, known as *zaboroly*, to protect soldiers from enemy arrows and later from artillery. In addition, the Kremlin gates were covered with iron, and a moat was dug around the walls. By the time construction was completed, Dmitry had also extended the Kremlin walls an additional 220 feet beyond the old oak walls, increasing not only the size of the fort but the size of the city as well. Thus, the boundaries had pushed to the north and east almost to the site of the present-day Kremlin.

The Black Plague hit Russia in the 1340s and caused many deaths, including that of Prince Simeon the Proud.

This new stone Kremlin stood not only as an impenetrable fortress but also as a symbol of the growing political importance of Moscow. The Kremlin's defensive strength offered its inhabitants more security than ever before, and it helped consolidate Prince Dmitry's authority over both the lesser nobility and the residents of Moscow. In time, the smaller principalities gathered under the Muscovite flag, unifying the region and affirming Moscow as a true capital city.

DEFENDING THE KREMLIN

The Kremlin not only appeared invincible, but it soon proved that it nearly was. In 1368, when the prince of Lithuania marched his army to the Kremlin walls, he did not even attempt to attack. Two years later, in 1370, the prince returned fully prepared to launch an offensive against the fort. For eight days he and his army attempted to penetrate the walls, but in the end they were unsuccessful.

In 1380 Dmitry scored yet another important triumph over the combined armies of the Lithuanians and the Tatars. Upon his return to the Kremlin, he marched in a great procession to the Cathedral of the Archangel Michael, where he stood solemnly before the tombs of his ancestors and gave thanks for his great victory. He then repeated the same ritual at the Cathedral of the Assumption.

Two years later, though, a more dangerous foe appeared at the city gates. In 1382 the Tatar khan Tokhtamysh, fueled by memories of the 1380 defeat suffered at the hands of Prince Dmitry, marched on the Kremlin. Prince Dmitry, away from the Kremlin to gather more firearms and men, was not there to protect his city. Inside the Kremlin walls, panic ensued as noblemen seeking to save themselves made plans to escape. The rest of Dmitry's subjects, however, demanded that the nobles stay and fight. When a group of noblemen did attempt to leave, fighting broke out. Several people died in the fray, but the nobles were prevented from leaving.

By the time the Tatars approached the walls, the Russians were ready. Confident of their ability to defend themselves from inside a fortress that they regarded as impenetrable, the Russians climbed to the top of the walls and taunted the attackers. Appalled by the audacity of their enemies, the Tatars tried for three days without success to breach the fortress.

Finally, Khan Tokhtamysh succeeded in doing what no one had managed to accomplish: He got inside the Kremlin. Sending a message to the Kremlin that he had no intention of causing any harm and wanted only some tribute, the khan waited. Finally, the gates of the Kremlin swung open, and a delegation of nobles rode out to meet him. As the procession left the safety of the fort behind them, the Tatars struck, killing all in the party. Others rushed through the open Kremlin gates or climbed over the walls on ladders that had been placed there for the attack.

ICONS AND THE ICONOSTASIS

The use of statues is forbidden in the Russian Orthodox Church, so Russians fill their churches with icons—that is, painted pictures that depict religious scenes and the lives of saints. For those of the Russian Orthodox faith, the presence of these special figures reminds them of the comfort the saints of the church provide. The iconostasis, a religious screen covered with icons, occupies a special place in the church and separates the people from the clergy. The screen also carries a symbolic meaning. When the screen's central, or "royal," door is opened and closed during the service, it signifies among other things the creation of the world and the birth and resurrection of Christ. Only priests and the czar during his coronation are allowed behind the door.

The iconostasis in the Cathedral of the Dormition separates the parishioners from the clergy.

Once inside, the Tatars burned the Kremlin, destroying everything within its confines, including valuable state papers and important government and personal documents belonging to Dmitry. In addition, the invaders massacred nearly twenty-four thousand people, from the very old to young children and even babies. Going about their work with a ruthless efficiency, the Tatars left few survivors among the smoldering ruins.

Once again, though, the surviving residents rebuilt the city and the Kremlin. On the ruins of the nobles' houses, new and even grander wooden and stone homes began to appear. One palace, belonging to a cousin of Prince Dmitry, was constructed of stone and included a beautiful mural that depicted the city of Moscow and its surrounding countryside. Even Dmitry's own home, which the Tatars had gutted, rose again, more magnificent than before.

By the time of Prince Dmitry's death in 1389, Moscow had emerged as the largest city in northeastern Russia, boasting a thriving regional and international center of trade. Moscow also maintained a strong religious identity since the hierarchy of the Russian Orthodox Church had maintained its operations within the Kremlin.

As vital and as thriving as Kalita's and Dmitry's city was, there is nothing left of it today. Fires, enemy attacks, looting, sieges, and time all took their toll on the medieval Kremlin. In the end, the expensive stone used to build the walls could not sustain the continual damage of war and the elements, and gradually the walls started to erode and collapse. Compounding the problem was the replacement of missing pieces of stone with wood, further weakening the walls. By the end of the fifteenth century, the wooden repairs were so extensive that one visitor thought the Kremlin walls were still made entirely of wood. It was a sad finale to the dream of building a great stone fortress.

3

UNMISTAKABLY RUSSIAN

On a cold November day in 1472, cheering crowds filled the snow-covered streets of Moscow. Many had come to catch a glimpse of the new princess, Sophia, who had journeyed all the way from Rome to marry their czar, Ivan III. Although some Russians voiced concern about the czar marrying a foreigner, especially one affiliated with the Roman Catholic Church, others pointed out that the soon-to-be czarina had agreed to convert to the Russian Orthodox faith, and perhaps, then, she deserved a chance.

The union of Ivan III and Sophia marked the beginning of a new and significant chapter in the history of Russia and the Kremlin. Ivan had long dreamed of building a sophisticated and resplendent capital and residence—dreams matched by the ambitions of his new wife. Sophia inspired and encouraged the extensive construction, and together the couple was instrumental in making the Kremlin one of the grandest and most significant architectural treasures in the world.

A CRUMBLING KREMLIN

By the mid–fifteenth century the Kreml Belokamennyl, or "Whitestone Kremlin," was falling down; the churches, palaces, and homes that had once graced the compound were shabby and dilapidated. Even as Russians came to acknowledge Moscow as their capital, and as a new ruler sat on the throne, city residents generally agreed that their Kremlin was no longer the glorious place it had been under Kalita and Prince Dmitry.

Yet the new czar, Ivan III (also known as Ivan the Great), was a strong ruler. Not only had he liberated his country from Tatar domination, but he had also annexed almost all of the independent principalities and cities in northern Russia. He had thereby extended the boundaries of his kingdom so that it encompassed Finland and the White Sea to the north and the Ural Mountains to the east.

Ivan, like his subjects, was dissatisfied with the current condition of the Kremlin. Urged by his wife, Ivan undertook a bold and innovative building program that promised to restore the former magnificence of the Kremlin and its buildings. He also was the first Muscovite prince to invite Western architects and engineers to work on the Kremlin.

THE ITALIANS

At first Ivan relied on the talents of local builders and engineers to carry out his ambitious plans. However, when a severe earthquake struck in 1472, destroying many buildings, Ivan was convinced that their skills were inadequate to the task. As a result, Ivan turned to the West, specifically to Italy, which was in the midst of the Renaissance, a period of cultural rebirth. Beginning in 1474 and continuing well into the sixteenth century, a number of Italian architects, jewelry makers, metalsmiths, and arms manufacturers made their way to Moscow to work at the Kremlin.

The work done on the Kremlin during this period is generally attributed to five Italian architects. Though there were oth-

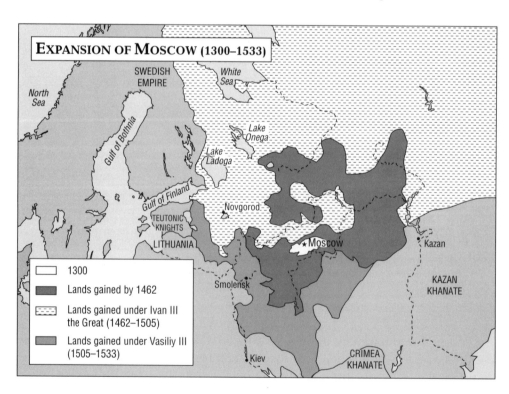

EXPANSION OF MOSCOW (1300–1533)

SWEDISH EMPIRE
White Sea
North Sea
Lake Onega
Gulf of Bothnia
Lake Ladoga
Gulf of Finland
Novgorod
TEUTONIC KNIGHTS
LITHUANIA
★ Moscow
Kazan
Smolensk
KAZAN KHANATE
Kiev
CRIMEA KHANATE

1300
Lands gained by 1462
Lands gained under Ivan III the Great (1462–1505)
Lands gained under Vasiliy III (1505–1533)

A BYZANTINE PRINCESS, A RUSSIAN QUEEN

If not for the influence of his wife, Sophia, Ivan III might never have devoted so much attention to the Kremlin. Spurred on by her insistence that he look to the West for architects and engineers, Ivan transformed the Kremlin into one of the world's true architectural masterpieces.

Sophia was both the niece of the last emperor of Byzantium and a daughter of Rome. As a young girl Sophia was sent to Rome as the ward of the pope; there, she was immediately attracted to the most vibrant and sophisticated Italian culture of the time. When she arrived in Moscow in 1475, she not only spoke her native Greek but had mastered Latin and Italian as well. She also brought with her books, manuscripts, artists, and architects. Hers was an influence that stretched far beyond the palace walls and, in fact, can still be seen in the Kremlin today.

ers who worked on the rebuilding and construction project, these are the ones about whom historians have the most information: Marco Ruffo, who came to Moscow in 1480; Antonio Friazin, who came in 1485; Pietro Antonio Solario, who arrived in 1490; Alevsio the Milanese (also called Alevsio Novyi), who appeared in 1494; and Ridolfo Fieravanti, called Aristotele, of Bologna, who arrived in 1475.

Of the five, Fieravanti is the one who stands out. He was not just an architect; he was also an engineer and an expert in military fortifications, metal casting, pyrotechnics (fireworks), and hydraulics. When an emissary of Ivan's approached him about going to Moscow, Fieravanti did not hesitate. In Russia, a land that many Westerners regarded as uncivilized, Fieravanti saw a great opportunity to express his vision and use his talents. Thus, in January 1475 he set out for Moscow, inspired by the dream of building a great city on the vast northern steppes.

A NEW BUILDING STYLE

Fieravanti and the Italian architects brought with them distinctly Italian building styles and techniques. As a result, much of the construction done during this time, especially on the Kremlin's fortifications (walls and towers), bears a strong resemblance to the palaces and townhouses found in northern Italy.

These fortifications, when finished, included places where the low walls jutted out, called bastions, and moats. The bastions were most often arrow-shaped, but they could also be rounded, rectangular, or polygonal. They helped protect the fortress because they gave defenders a strategic advantage over enemies below. Likewise, the moats were often surrounded by a double, and sometimes triple, system of walls that made it difficult for invaders to mount a successful attack. This design was a revolutionary breakthrough in fortification architecture and became a standard for city defense systems well into the eighteenth century.

REBUILDING BEGINS

Given the size and scope of the project, the Italians decided first to build a plant to manufacture bricks on-site rather than have them brought in. They also taught local workmen and builders a number of Western building techniques, including how to make a better type of mortar—the substance used to bond the bricks together.

Then, in the spring of 1485, construction began on the south walls facing the Moskva River, thought to be the most vulnerable to attack. During the next fourteen years the Italian architects continued to reconstruct the Kremlin's walls and towers on all sides. They had workmen excavate and drain the area, removing portions of the walls and rebuilding the Kremlin's foundations. But upon reaching the north end of the Kremlin, which faced the Neglinnaya River, the Italians found they had a serious problem.

Before the walls and towers could be built, the riverbanks needed to be reinforced so that they could support the new, heavier walls. In order to do this properly, an extensive strip of land, measuring almost 760 feet, had to be cleared away. This undertaking involved more than simply removing dirt. The workers had to dig up portions of an existing graveyard, some churches, and homes. The clergy and nobles were outraged and protested to the czar. But seeing the need for the new walls, Ivan ordered the work to proceed.

In constructing the new walls, the Italian architects and engineers introduced the Russians to a new building material: bricks.

The individual bricks on average weighed 40 kilograms, the equivalent of nine modern bricks, and measured roughly 12 inches long, about 5.5 inches wide, and 7 inches thick. The bricks were then laid in a vertical pattern, opposed to the more traditional horizontal, side-by-side pattern that most brick structures used. The Italians now used the white stone, which had formerly served as the primary building material, to form the bases of the walls and for decorative purposes. Instead of massive, ponderous walls of stone, the new brick walls and towers of the Italian-style Kremlin appeared lighter and more delicate. In fact, though, they were stronger, more stable, and less prone to erosion.

At last, in 1499, the walls were finished and the area of the Kremlin had grown to its present size of 65.5 acres. The fortress now offered an impressive sight. As a French observer once wrote,

> How am I to describe the walls of the Kremlin? The word *wall* gives an idea of quite too ordinary an object; it would deceive the reader: the walls of the Kremlin are a chain of mountains. This citadel, reared on the confines of Europe and Asia, is, compared with ordinary ramparts what the Alps are to our hills; the Kremlin is the Mount Blanc [the largest mountain in France] of fortresses.[7]

THE TOWERS OF THE KREMLIN

The Italians also rebuilt the Kremlin's towers, once again drawing on the styles of their homeland. This included building the towers of brick as well as making each one slightly different from the others. All of the towers, with the exception of the Arsenal Tower, are cylindrical in shape. Each has a white-stone base with a decorative

The Beklemishev Tower (pictured), along with the Kremlin's other towers, was rebuilt by Italian architects who drew on the architectural styles of their homeland.

band encircling it. Atop the base is a two-tiered main section, also called a superstructure, which consists of a circular lower tier and an octagonal upper tier.

The first tower the Italians built was the Tainitskaia, or "Secret Tower," in 1485. Designed by Antonio Friazin, the tower stands 126 feet high. At the time, it served as a gate tower and also contained an underground well. In the event that the Kremlin fell under siege and the inhabitants needed water, a secret passage led to the Moskva River.

The Corner Arsenal Tower followed in 1492. Built by Pietro Antonio Solario, this tower is the most commanding of all of the Kremlin towers. Although set on a white-stone base like the others, the main section of the Corner Arsenal Tower is a polyhedron, or sixteen-sided space, with walls that are thirteen feet thick. The tower is 168 feet wide, stands more than 200 feet tall, and covers the only working underground reservoir left in the Kremlin. The upper section of the tower is encircled with numerous machicolations, or special overhangs commonly built at the top of medieval forts. Within these overhangs, floor openings

Built in 1492 by Pietro Antonio Solario, the Corner Arsenal Tower is 168 feet wide, more than 200 feet tall, and has walls that are thirteen feet thick.

THE IVAN THE GREAT BELL TOWER

Located in the center of Cathedral Square is the Ivan the Great Bell Tower. Built between 1505 and 1508 by Ivan's son Vasily III as a tribute to his father, the Ivan the Great Bell Tower is the tallest structure in the Kremlin, standing 266 feet high. Three hundred and twenty-nine steps lead to the top, where the view extends for almost 25 miles. The structure was an ideal watchtower, used for centuries. If a sentinel sighted an enemy approaching, he could sound the bells, alerting residents to come to the defense of their city. Throughout the course of Russian history, the Ivan the Great Bell Tower has stood firm, evidence of its exceptional strength and the skill of its builders.

For centuries, the 266-foot-high Ivan the Great Bell Tower was an ideal watchtower.

were made through which cauldrons of boiling oil could be poured on attackers. This tower's construction also completed the Kremlin's line of defense on the Red Square side.

THE GATE TOWERS

In addition, five entrance, or gate, towers are located throughout the Kremlin: the Spasskia, or "Saviour's"; the Troitskia, or "Trinity"; the Nikol'skaia, or "St. Nicholas"; the Borovitskaia, or "Forest"; and the Tainitskaia, or "Secret Gate." To enter the Kremlin, people must pass through one of these gates.

Numerous architectural historians consider the Saviour's Gate to be the most exceptional of the five. Located on the east side of the Kremlin, the Saviour's Gate has served as the fortress's formal entrance for more than five centuries.

Having served as a formal entrance for more than five centuries, Saviour's Gate is considered by many historians to be the Kremlin's most exceptional gate tower.

Originally, the gate was known as the Frolov Gate. However, at some point an image of Christ was painted on the wall above the entrance, and the gate became known as the Saviour's Gate. In homage, a beautiful lantern was hung in front of the image, where devotional candles were always kept lit. All ceremonial processions, from the coronation of czars to religious celebrations, passed through this gate, as did soldiers departing to or returning from war. For many Russian royals and nobles, the last journey they ever made was through the Saviour's Gate on their way to be buried.

THE KREMLIN PALACES

In addition to walls and towers, the Italians also designed palaces for the czar. At the top of Kremlin Hill is the site picked by Russia's rulers for their home, and in 1487 Ivan III commissioned Italian architect Marco Ruffo to build a new palace there.

This building, known as the Palace of the Facets, received its name from the diamond-shaped white stones that cover the outside of its east wall. The Palace of the Facets served Ivan and his court as a formal location to receive guests and to conduct government business. Today it is the oldest government building in the city of Moscow. Originally, a white-stone porch decorated with ornate carvings connected the palace with the nearby Church of the Holy Vestibule, but it has since been destroyed.

The Palace of the Facets took four years to build and shows the influence of its Italian architecture in its resemblance to Italy's elegant Renaissance palaces. The palace is a large two-story, square building. The ground floor holds storerooms, and the upper floor houses a large ceremonial hall, which is seventy feet by seventy-seven feet. The hall receives light from eighteen windows on three of the walls. At night the hall is lit by four massive round bronze chandeliers. The walls were later covered with a number of beautiful murals that illustrated both religious and historical themes. The royal throne once stood on the south side of the hall. On the west wall, near the ceiling, was a curtained

THE FIRST ENTRANCE GATE

One of the most distinct of the five entrance gates at the Kremlin is the Borovitskaia, or "Forest Gate," located along the west wall. The only gate entrance without a tower, the Forest Gate is distinguished by its massive base, four stepped levels, arched entrance, and green-tiled steeple. Built in 1490, the gate is thought to mark the original entrance to the Kremlin. Experts believe that merchants, tradesmen, and farmers may have used the gate on a daily basis, for some of the original structures located near it housed a granary and a stable area rather than official government buildings. From its earliest days, the gate also had a drawbridge that people used to cross over the Neglinnaya River. Today the only signs of the drawbridge are the old slots where the chains used to lower and raise the bridge. The gate also has the dubious honor of being the entrance that Napoléon Bonaparte used when he entered Moscow in 1812.

opening where members of the royal family could watch the goings-on without being seen.

Of all of the Kremlin's palaces and rooms, this hall at the Palace of the Facets was probably the best known. Countless descriptions of the hall, written by foreign diplomats, have survived. A visitor to the Russian royal court once wrote,

> The hall was large enough, but in the center was a large column which supported the vault and diminished its beauty very much. Old paintings were on the walls, to which were attached silver plaques between two windows. Around the room were benches built against the wall, covered with carpets, and approached by steps. . . . It was difficult to see the Tsar [czar], seated on a silver-gilt throne, placed not in the center, but in the left corner of the hall between two windows.[8]

THE TEREM PALACE

At the end of the fifteenth century, Ivan III began planning the construction of new living quarters, which would be called the

The Palace of the Facets received its name from the diamond-shaped white stones that decorate the exterior of its east wall.

ROUGHING IT

Many Russian rulers did not sleep in their palaces. Instead, they left the comforts of their royal residences for days, weeks, or even months in search of the simple life in poor peasant huts or the local monasteries. Many times, circumstances forced them to leave their palaces. Ivan III, for example, fled after a fire destroyed portions of the Kremlin in 1493. Despite the beauty and delicacy of the Italian architecture, other czars and nobles preferred the traditional wooden structures of their ancestors. In the book *The Kremlin: Eight Centuries of Tyranny and Terror*, author Jules Koslow quotes one seventeenth-century visitor to Moscow on the preferences of one royal father and son: "There is lately built a very fair place of stone, according to the Italian architecture for the young Prince, but the Great Duke continues still in his wooden palace, as being more healthy than stone structures."

Terem Palace. Years earlier, one of his homes had been destroyed by fire, and for some time he was forced to live in the simple quarters of a peasant until his home could be rebuilt.

Supervised by Italian architect Alevisio Novyi, construction of the Terem Palace began in 1499 at the top of Kremlin Hill, the site of earlier royal residences. To improve security for the royal family, Ivan also ordered the construction of a masonry wall to protect the home and its inhabitants from danger. Finally, in 1503, the palace was finished. Under the watchful eye of Novyi, it had turned out every bit as sumptuous as the Palace of the Facets. In the upper stories were located the bedchambers of the czar as well as his waiting rooms, where boyars and the czar's advisers congregated.

IVAN'S CHURCHES

Although Ivan III, and after him his son Vasily III, allowed the Kremlin's walls, towers, and palaces to have a decidedly Italian influence, the cathedrals were another matter. Here, the architects followed the prevailing Russian style of church architecture, a style heavily influenced by the Byzantine tradition. Thus, the Russian Cathedrals featured large, ornate domes, elaborately

POLYCHROME ARCHITECTURE

Polychrome architecture consisted of applying multicolored materials to create patterns. Whether it was different colored bricks or stone, painted wood, or the application of glazes or enamel paints, the effect was often breathtaking.

Enamel covering, in particular, became a Russian trademark. The enamel—a very tough and durable paint coating—not only provided the brick or wood protection from the elements, but it also allowed craftsmen the opportunity to experiment with striking patterns, colors, and surfaces.

carved columns, and a dizzying array of decorative elements such as round arches and rich colors.

The cathedrals are situated around Cathedral Square, an area that became the social and political center of Moscow during Ivan the Great's reign. The main streets of the Kremlin meet here, and the square was the site of many magnificent and festive ceremonies throughout Russian history. In the square are grouped three of the most magnificent churches in the world: the Cathedral of the Dormition, the Cathedral of the Annunciation, and the Cathedral of the Archangel Michael. These cathedrals are so spectacular that one historian described them as being the "Russian counterparts of Reims, Saint Denis, and Sainte Chapelle [three famous French cathedrals]."[9]

THE CATHEDRAL OF THE DORMITION

The Cathedral of the Dormition is the Kremlin's most celebrated church. From the fifteenth century on, this was where the Russian czars, after receiving their crowns, placed a copy of their last will and testament inside a silver casket. It is also the location of the canopied wooden throne used as the coronation chair. In addition, the highest-ranking members of the Russian Orthodox clergy are buried here. Despite its size (it is one of the smallest churches in Cathedral Square), its connection with Russian history makes the Cathedral of the Dormition loom large in the Russian imagination.

Although this cathedral was begun in 1326, during the reign of Ivan Kalita, by 1475 the church was badly in need of repair. To supervise the renovation, Ivan the Great called again on Italian architect Ridolfo Fieravanti. From the outset, Ivan made one thing clear: The church was to look like a Russian, not a Western, church. Ivan even suggested that Fieravanti travel throughout the country to see what other great Russian churches looked like.

Fieravanti took his patron's advice, visiting a number of churches and monasteries, taking careful note not only of those constructed of wood but also those built of stone. He returned to Moscow, and in the spring of 1475 he began work on the Cathedral of the Dormition.

To rebuild, though, Fieravanti first had to destroy. He razed the remaining walls of the earlier cathedral, which had fallen into severe disrepair. As one architectural historian later described the scene: "Muscovites were startled to see what had taken three years to build dismantled, with the Italians' technological ingenuity, in a week."[10]

By June 1475 construction began in earnest on the foundation of the new church. Placed on oak piles, or supports, the stone foundation walls were set at a depth of thirteen feet—the deepest ever dug in Russia for a foundation wall—which would stabilize the church walls more securely than they had been before. Fieravanti also had a brickworks constructed so that workmen could manufacture large bricks, stronger than any he had ever used.

The cupolas, or domes, of the Cathedral of the Dormition represent Christ and the four Evangelists.

During construction Fieravanti incorporated elements often found in Russian churches. For instance, he added five cupolas, or domes—a common architectural element in Russian churches —with each one symbolizing some religious aspect. In this case, the five domes of the Cathedral of the Dormition represented Christ and the four Evangelists who wrote the Gospels: Matthew, Mark, Luke, and John.

Fieravanti also incorporated into the design some innovations of his own. He did away with the choir galleries, which gave the church a more open and expansive feel. He made use of stronger supports and thereby avoided the heavy masonry that had to be used in earlier Russian churches to bolster their tremendous weight.

Upon completion, one of the cathedral's most magnificent treasures was its iconostasis, a special screen on which icons, or paintings representing the saints of the Russian Orthodox Church, were placed. The iconostasis covered an entire wall with one of the most fabulous displays of Russian icons in the country. The icons were encased in gold, wore breastplates of gold and silver, and had haloes adorned with thousands of precious jewels.

The cathedral was a marvel, so beautiful, in fact, that when Ivan, church officials, and noblemen visited the newly finished church, they exclaimed, "We see heaven!"[11] The Cathedral of the Dormition set the standard for Russian churches for years to come.

THE CATHEDRAL OF THE ANNUNCIATION

The next church that Ivan the Great commissioned was the Cathedral of the Annunciation, also known as the Royal Chapel of the Czars. Built by Russian architects between 1484 and 1489,

Built between 1484 and 1489, the Cathedral of the Annunciation became a popular place of worship for Russian royal women.

the cathedral was small and crowned with only three domes. In time, the Cathedral of the Annunciation became the favorite worshiping place of the Russian royal women, who preferred its intimate atmosphere.

The interior of the church, though small, did not lack in grandeur. Four rectangular pillars support the vaulted ceiling.

Although the interior of the Cathedral of the Annunciation provides a more intimate atmosphere than some of the Kremlin's other cathedrals, it does not lack grandeur.

Along the west wall is a choir gallery where the czarina and her children participated in services. Like the Cathedral of the Dormition, one of the most remarkable pieces in the Cathedral of the Annunciation is its iconostasis, which consisted of five tiers, stood fifty-two feet high, and dated from the early fifteenth century. The display was so grand that one clergyman was moved to write,

> No goldsmith could evaluate the great stones, diamonds, emeralds, rubies, set upon the icons and haloes of Our Saviour and Our Lady. The jewels glow in the darkness like coals. The gilding of the icons was pure gold. Many-hued enamels executed the finest art and aroused the admiration of the discerning observer. The value of the icons in the church would fill several treasuries.[12]

THE CATHEDRAL OF THE ARCHANGEL MICHAEL

Resting on the foundation of an earlier church is Ivan the Great's Cathedral of the Archangel Michael, constructed in the first years of the sixteenth century. Built by Italian architect Alevisio Noyvi, the cathedral is a rectangular structure with five domes.

Unlike the other Kremlin cathedrals, though, the Cathedral of the Archangel had silver rather than gold domes.

The Cathedral of the Archangel is special because it is the burial place of the czars. Here rest all of the Russian princes, grand princes, and czars since Ivan Kalita (with the exception of Nicholas II, now interred in St. Petersburg). Each ruler was buried in a brass-covered coffin; on top of each is a painted figure wearing a halo and a long, white robe. Altogether there are forty-six tombs containing the remains of fifty-two individuals.

THE END OF AN ERA

The influence of the Italian architects lasted little more than a century because, despite their willingness to work for the czars, the Italians came to be mistrusted. They were, after all, Roman Catholics. Despite the pope's overtures toward improving relations between the Orthodox and Roman churches, many Russian clergy feared that the Italians were secretly trying to undermine the influence of the Russian Orthodox Church. In the early sixteenth century, therefore, the Russians sent the Italians on their way.

The Italians may have left the Kremlin, but their influence remained. The Kremlin was no longer a hulking mass of white stone and wood; instead, it was a stylish and functional fortress with double and triple walls of red brick, studded with towers, spires, and drawbridges. Protected by these seemingly unbreachable walls were the newly built palaces, cathedrals, and homes, also part of the Italian legacy. The appearance of these buildings, writes one architectural historian, with "their shining cupolas, the elegant palaces, picturesque *terema* [houses] with their observation platforms, lanterns [a windowed tower], and varicolored roofs gave the fortress the appearance of a fairy-tale town."[13]

With the help of his Italian architects, artisans, and engineers, Ivan the Great embarked on a systematic plan to transform the Kremlin from, in the words of one scholar, "the primitive character of an ancient Russian city to . . . the appearance of a European citadel [fortress]."[14] In building his new palaces, churches, towers, and walls, Ivan did not intend merely to provide for his comfort and safety. Rather, he also sought to advertise Moscow as a commercial, artistic, cultural, and political center and to demonstrate to foreign visitors and rivals the power, wealth, and importance of his kingdom.

THE KREMLIN IN TURMOIL

Ivan III died in 1505. Under his rule, the Russians had finally overthrown the hated Tatar invaders and extended the borders of the Russian Empire. Gradually, the Russian states were becoming unified under a single ruler, with Moscow as the cultural, religious, and political capital. At the center of the city, the kingdom, and the empire was Ivan's masterpiece: the Kremlin.

In the centuries following Ivan's death, the Kremlin would serve as the stage for a number of dramatic events in Russian history. And once again, after the wars were fought and the fires put out, the Kremlin stood more splendid than before.

VASILY III

Ivan's son Vasily became czar in 1505. Unlike his father, Vasily was cold and ruthless, crushing those who opposed his ideas or his will. Like his father, Vasily also wished to extend the boundaries of the Russian Empire and to make Russia less isolated from the rest of western Europe. To that end, he permitted some western Europeans to enter the country. However, Vasily watched the foreigners carefully, as he was not willing for his country to come completely under the influence of Western ways and styles.

During his reign, Vasily continued the work begun by his father to both beautify and fortify the Kremlin. In 1508 he ordered a new moat dug around the fortress, telling the Italian architect Alevesio the Milanese "to dig a ditch along the east side of the Kremlin wall, face [cover] its banks with stone and brick, dam up the Neglinnaya River and build reservoirs around the town [the Kremlin]."[15] Following the czar's instructions, Alevesio dug a moat that ranged in depth from 31 to 42 feet and measured anywhere from 100 to 142 feet wide. Low walls rose on either side of the moat, and there were two drawbridges, one located at the north entrance gate and the other at the south. Vasily also ordered additional construction to strengthen the Kremlin walls.

Along the Moskva River side, an additional wall of brick was built, as well as more towers.

Inside the Kremlin walls, Vasily started a number of building projects and altered some existing structures. Two of the new buildings were religious: the Church of St. John the Baptist and the Ascension Convent, which housed about thirty nuns. The convent was also the final resting place of the Russian grand princesses and czarinas until the middle of the nineteenth century.

IVAN THE TERRIBLE

Named grand prince at the age of three, Vasily's son and Ivan III's grandson, Ivan Grozny, who later became known as Ivan the Terrible, grew up in the Kremlin. At the age of sixteen, Ivan told his advisers that he did not wish to be crowned "grand prince" of Russia, as his predecessors had been. He would take a new and more important title: czar and autocrat of all Russia. Although Ivan's pronouncement stunned his advisers, they did not oppose him out of fear for their lives, and, in January 1547, the metropolitan of the Russian Orthodox Church crowned Ivan Grozny as Czar Ivan IV.

Ivan the Terrible was crowned czar of Russia in 1547.

That same year also saw another catastrophic fire in Moscow. A strong wind whipped the flames, quickly spreading the fire throughout the city. According to one historian's description, when it was over, Moscow lay in ashes and resembled

an immense funeral pile, over which was spread a pall of thick and black smoke. The wooden edifices disappeared entirely. Those of stone and brick presented a still more gloomy aspect, with only portions of their walls standing, crumbling and blackened. The howling of the tempest, the roar of the flames, the crash of falling buildings, and the shrieks of the inhabitants, were all fre-

THE CZAR

The title *czar*, derived from the imperial Roman title *caesar*, is associated primarily with rulers of Russia, but it was not always this way. In medieval Russia the title *czar* referred to a supreme ruler, particularly the Byzantine emperor, who was the head of the Orthodox Christian world. The fall of the Byzantine Empire in 1453 and the Ottoman Turks' subsequent conquest of the Balkans, however, left the grand princes of Moscow the only remaining Orthodox monarchs. Thus, the Russian Orthodox clergy began to look to the grand princes as the chief defenders and supreme heads of Orthodox Christianity. In 1547 Ivan IV, grand prince of Moscow, was officially crowned czar of all Russia, and thus the religious and political ideology of the Russian czardom took its final form.

The word had always held a special connotation for Ivan. He discovered the word *czar* while reading about the early rulers of the ancient world, and he noted that it meant "supreme power." He believed that the title would not only set to rest any question about who ruled Russia, but it would also convey the historic ties of the throne to Byzantium and to Rome.

As czar, Ivan IV theoretically held absolute power. In practice, though, he and his successors were limited by the traditional authority of the Orthodox church, the boyar council, special legal codes, and their limited resources.

quently overpowered by the explosions of the powder magazines in the arsenal of the Kremlin.[16]

The damage to the city was immense; the damage to the Kremlin was just as severe. The winds had carried the deadly embers over the brick walls of the fortress. The interior of the Cathedral of the Assumption suffered terrible damage, as did the czar's palace and the Cathedral of the Annunciation. The armory buildings were completely destroyed, as were the homes of the metropolitan and many Russian nobles. Gone forever were the religious relics, the priceless royal treasures, and the beautiful frescoes that had decorated the walls of the churches.

Ivan and his family fled the devastation, taking refuge at a royal residence outside the city. As soon as the fire was over, Ivan gave orders for work to begin to restore the Kremlin. For the next year, the Kremlin and the city of Moscow rose once more from the ashes.

THE CATHEDRAL OF ST. BASIL THE BLESSED

Between the years 1552 and 1556, Ivan defeated the two main Tatar strongholds, the khanate, or state, of Kazan and the khanate of Astrakhan. Only the khanate of the Crimea to the south of Moscow remained to be conquered. Ivan's advisers implored him to move at once to finish off the Tatars. He rejected their counsel, however, believing that the region was too well fortified and that an attack against the Tatars in the Crimea might provoke the Turks to invade Russia. Instead, to commemorate the victories he had already won and to celebrate the triumph of Christianity over Islam, Ivan ordered the construction of the Church of the Intercession of the Virgin (Pokrovskii Sobor), better known as the Cathedral of St. Basil the Blessed, at Red Square, a large oblong rectangle located outside the Kremlin walls that was the center of political, social, and economic life in medieval Russia.

Ivan the Terrible ordered the Cathedral of St. Basil the Blessed to be built to commemorate what he viewed as the triumph of Christianity over Islam.

In 1571, though, the Tatars attacked Moscow and the Kremlin once more. They especially concentrated their wrath in Red Square, and particularly on St. Basil's because the church commemorated the Russians' earlier victory over them and, as a result, had significant symbolic importance to the Russian people. By the end of the rampage, the

Tatars had killed at least one hundred thousand Muscovites, with some estimates of the Russian dead ranging as high as eight hundred thousand.

But the Cathedral of St. Basil (Khram Vasoliia Blazhennago) survived the Tatar onslaught. Built between 1553 and 1560, the cathedral stands atop a steep incline at the end of Vasilievskaia Street in the southeast corner of Red Square. St. Basil's is actually the dominant structure in a complex of eight churches, each one dedicated to a saint whose feast day coincided with one of Ivan's eight victories over the Tatars.

St. Basil's occupies an exceptional place in Russian architectural history. The cathedral, with each of its ten domes differing in design and color, is gaudy and ornate, bursting with color and composed of different shapes. Long the subject of furious debates among architectural historians, St. Basil's has been both ridiculed as "the dream of a diseased imagination"[17] and praised as an expression of Russian genius.

WHO REALLY DESIGNED ST. BASIL'S?

Legend has it that an Italian architect designed and built St. Basil's. When he had finished his work, he was blinded by order of the czar so that he could never produce a more beautiful church elsewhere. In another version of the legend, the czar asked the architect if he could ever build a more magnificent church. When the architect replied that he could, the czar ordered him beheaded so that St. Basil's would remain forever unrivaled. The actual history of St. Basil's, although somewhat less colorful, in no way diminishes the grandeur of this extraordinary edifice.

Designed by the Russian architects Barma and Posnik Iakovlev, the Cathedral of St. Basil the Blessed is constructed of stone and brick and is covered with stucco. Originally white, during the seventeenth century the structure was painted a combination of red, orange, yellow, green, blue, violet, gold, and silver. The interior, by contrast, is dark, somber, and cavernous, although frescoes were added in 1784.

The most striking characteristics of St. Basil's are its elaborate steeples, each topped with an onion-shaped cupola. The eight main cupolas are each topped by a central pyramid-shaped spire and are of the same general size and shape, but each has a different design. Some cupolas are twisted and variegated, and others are decorated with ribbed patterns. Still others are faceted and spiny, giving the appearance of gigantic pineapples. The lavish use of colored tile heightened the diversity of form among the cupolas. Although highly individual in character, the cupolas somehow combine to form a harmonious whole. Nineteenth-century European travelers, astonished by the ensemble of steeples and cupolas, compared them to "a bush, a plant, or a bouquet of vari-colored flowers."[18]

AN AMBITIOUS BUILDING PROGRAM

In the tradition of his father and grandfather, Ivan IV carried on an ambitious building program for the Kremlin. In addition to the construction of St. Basil's, he commissioned four single-domed chapels to be added to the main church of the Cathedral of the Annunciation. All of the domes were gilded; together they formed a pyramid silhouetted against the sky. A white-stone porch was also added around the same time, setting an example that other Russian churches followed.

Ivan also found distinct uses for some of the Kremlin towers. The smallest of the towers, the Czar Tower, received its name because Ivan used it as a vantage point from which to watch public executions. And the Annunciation Tower, which was built during 1487 and 1488 and was once used as a laundry, Ivan pressed into service as a prison.

THE TIME OF TROUBLES

On March 28, 1584, while playing a game of chess, Ivan IV collapsed and died. His death plunged Russia into seventy years of political strife known as the Time of Troubles.

Due to the unrest, there was little done in the way of building at the Kremlin. The only significant structure constructed was the Ivan the Great Bell Tower, completed during the brief reign of Boris Godunov (1598–1605).

Colorful and lavishly decorated onion domes, each with its own design, crown the Cathedral of St. Basil.

THE SECRET LIBRARY

Despite Ivan the Terrible's reputation as one of the worst tyrants in history, he was also a man of culture and learning. Even as a youngster Ivan had a deep interest in antiquity, and he ultimately became a collector of both Russian and foreign manuscripts. Ivan knew that he was amassing a valuable collection and took great steps to preserve it. Well aware of the dangers that living in the Kremlin posed, he sought a way to protect his books and manuscripts from fire, theft, and vandalism. Thus, he ordered the construction of secret vaults beneath the Kremlin in which to store his precious texts—vaults he eventually ordered sealed.

Unfortunately, no one today knows where the vaults are located. Although several attempts have been made over the years to locate Ivan's secret library, it remains hidden, perhaps forever.

After Godunov's death, a series of imposters claiming ties to the Russian royal family descended on the Kremlin, and the political situation rapidly moved toward chaos. The Russian nobility took sides with the various pretenders to the throne, the serfs openly rebelled against their masters, and gangs of bandits roamed throughout the countryside looting and pillaging.

THE POLISH INVASION

Amid this backdrop of violence and confusion, the Poles attacked and captured the Kremlin. In 1611 Polish troops marched into Moscow and through the Kremlin gates. The once impenetrable fortress was invincible no more. The Poles controlled the Kremlin for the next two years.

During the Polish occupation the Kremlin suffered a great deal of damage from both Polish vandalism and Russian shelling. The Ivan the Great Bell Tower was partially destroyed, and several of the palaces had gaping holes in their roofs and shattered glass from their windows. The Poles either stole, destroyed, or mutilated precious works of art, concentrating especially on disfiguring religious art and relics to express their hatred of the Russian Orthodox Church.

THE KRASNAYA PLOSHCHAD

Red Square is among the most recognized sites in the world. For hundreds of years, many important events in Russian history have unfolded on this majestic square, which flanks the west wall of the Kremlin. Commerce, religious and military parades and pageants, public torture and execution, political rallies, war, and revolution—Red Square has witnessed them all. *Krasnaya*, the Old Russian word for "red," also means "beautiful." It is from this dual meaning that the Red Square, or Krasnaya Ploshchad, gets its name.

Russian soldiers march during a 1999 military parade in Red Square.

Here was located the Lobnoe Mesto, or "Place of the Skull," a low stone platform from which the medieval czars addressed their subjects and the patriarchs of the Russian Orthodox Church blessed the faithful. Crowds mingled in Red Square to hear town criers relate the latest news or to listen as the heralds of the czar announced new *ukazy*, or "edicts." People came, also, to socialize and conduct business, for Red Square was, among other things, a sprawling and vibrant marketplace.

Red Square was also the scene of other, less savory activities, such as public torture and execution. In Red Square, criminals and enemies of the czars were brought to be beaten, hanged, beheaded, impaled, broken on the wheel, or burned at the stake.

Finally, in 1613, the Russians, under the leadership of a butcher from Novgorod and a nobleman, raised an army and marched on the Kremlin. After bitter fighting, they ousted the Poles and retook the Kremlin. The Polish invasion marked the first time in history that foreigners held the Kremlin. The Russians swore it would never happen again.

Abandoned and Rescued

In the summer of 1613, the Zemsky Sobor, or "National Assembly," nominated sixteen-year-old Michael Romanov to rule Russia. Romanov had a legitimate claim to the throne: He was a grandnephew of one of Ivan IV's wives. His family had also tried to maintain order during the Time of Troubles, and Romanov himself was too young to have been involved in the political upheavals of the period. All in all, he seemed like a good choice.

Romanov's election to the throne was unanimous, and on July 11, 1613, Michael I was crowned the new czar of Russia in a ceremony held at the Cathedral of the Assumption. His ascension to the throne marked the beginning of the Romanov rule, which lasted for three hundred years.

Michael's reign as czar was, for the most part, unremarkable. However, during the reign of the Romanovs, the Kremlin finally received the much-needed repairs that would fix the damage done during the Time of Troubles. When they could at last afford to do so, Michael and his successors also went to great lengths to beautify the Kremlin.

The New Face of the Kremlin

Among the improvements that Michael Romanov carried out were the whitewashing of the Kremlin's brick walls and the building of two additional towers. Michael also ordered that one of the original Kremlin towers, the Saviour's Tower, undergo an extensive renovation in 1625.

To supervise the work, Michael invited Christopher Galloway to come to Russia and work at the Kremlin. Galloway, an Englishman with a good reputation as a designer and an architect, first replaced the original battlements of the Saviour's Tower with an even grander structure, which included galleries, balconies, and parapets. On top of this rose a splendid octagonal bell tower, with a windowed tower above it. Capping the new construction was a narrow spire.

In redoing the Saviour's Tower, Galloway combined a number of different styles in the tower design. Ornately decorated turrets and columns adorn the tower while grotesque gargoyles peer through the railings. Niches, or small recesses in the tower walls, held sculptured figures clothed in colorful costumes. The tower also contained a number of secret passageways, many of which have never been completely explored.

During this time, the Romanovs also ordered the construction of several new churches, including the Cathedral of the Twelve Apostles, built in 1655 and located on the north side of Cathedral Square, and the Church of the Resurrection, built in 1681. In addition, new living quarters for the patriarch, the head of the Russian Orthodox Church, were constructed in 1650. Known as the Palace of the Patriarchs, the building housed some of the finest collections of religious art in the entire country.

RECONSTRUCTING THE TEREM PALACE

In 1635 Michael ordered a group of Russian master builders to refurbish the Terem Palace, constructing the new building on top of the surviving ground and first floors of the original, which had been built by Ivan III. After a series of fires in 1547 and 1571 and the almost total destruction of the palace by the Poles in 1610, the Terem Palace was in terrible condition.

Many historians considered the Terem Palace the most splendid Kremlin residence, and it stands as the best-preserved residential complex in the Kremlin. It is a showcase of the Russian architectural style, utilizing the brick and polychrome—that is, the brightly colored enamel—techniques native to the country. Built of brick and painted a bright red, the palace is five stories high, with glazed red-and-white diamond-shaped roof tiles and white-stone carved decorations. A pavilion, or upper floor apartment, with an observation deck (traditionally used by the women of the royal family) is situated on the palace roof. Carved stonework depicting birds, foliage, and mythical beasts painted in bright colors adorns the building. Furthermore, all of the windows and doors of the palace are decorated with luxurious wood carvings that make each a truly unique piece of art.

The interiors of the Terem Palace are also spectacular. Square in shape, with vaulted ceilings throughout, the palace rooms are breathtaking. Painted walls were covered with either frescoes, gold gilding, or gilded leather. Polish artisans brought in to work

The interior of the Terem Palace is adorned with vaulted ceilings, painted walls, and gold gilding.

on the palace embedded precious metals and jewels into the ceilings. Beautifully tiled stoves heated the rooms. Expensive velvet covered the benches, and numerous carpets lay on the floors. New conveniences, including cupboards, bookcases, and expensive furniture from the West, added further adornment to the palace. One of the most breathtaking decorations in the Terem Palace was the ceiling in the czar's formal dining room, which was painted to represent, according to one historian, "with astronomical accuracy the solar system and the fixed stars."[19]

THE CZAR CANNON AND BELL

During the reign of the Romanovs, two curiosities were also added to the Kremlin that have, in time, attracted more attention than even the palaces or churches. The first is the Czar Cannon, an exquisite example of sixteenth-century foundry work. The bronze cannon was cast in 1586 and weighs nearly forty tons. It has a barrel that is seventeen feet long and a bore, or opening, that is thirty-five inches wide, making it the largest bore of any cannon in the world. Its ornate carriage and the cannon balls lined up near it are decorative and were cast of pig iron in 1835 at

Built in 1568, the Czar Cannon boasts the largest bore of any cannon in the world.

The Czar Bell measures twenty feet high and is covered with relief representations of Czar Alexis I and Empress Anna Ivanovna.

the ironworks in St. Petersburg. The cannon was never intended for actual use; instead, it was considered a great work of art.

The second curiosity, resting on a granite base at the foot of the Ivan the Great Bell Tower, is the largest bell in the world: the Czar Bell. The bell stands 20 feet high, has a diameter at the base of 22 feet, weighs 216 tons, and is made of just under 80 percent copper. It was cast in the Kremlin between 1733 and 1735. Russian master craftsmen skillfully adorned the surface of the bell with relief representations of the second Romanov czar, Alexis I, and the empress Anna Ivanovna (reigned 1730–1740). Five icons and two inscriptions are also found on the bell.

In 1737 a fire swept through Moscow, engulfing the Kremlin.

THE AMUSEMENT PALACE

One of the most interesting royal residences in the Kremlin is the Poteshnyi Dvorets, or the "Amusement Palace." Built sometime in the mid–seventeenth century, the palace was originally the home of a wealthy boyar, Ilia Miloslavsky. After his death, Czar Alexis I ordered the home remodeled as a theater. Beginning in 1672, the Amusement Palace was used for theatrical performances and other amusements to entertain the czar and his family.

The flames heated the metal bell, and when water was poured on the hot bell to cool it, it cracked. As a result, an 11.5-ton piece broke off.

A PERIOD OF DECLINE

Between 1680 and 1690 the Kremlin continued to undergo extensive construction. Stone passageways, both covered and open; hanging gardens; new roofs; and other additions to the churches and towers were completed, and by the beginning of the eighteenth century the Kremlin had reached the summit of its beauty, power, and prestige. But with the ascent to the throne of Peter the Great and his half-brother Ivan in 1682, the Kremlin's status as the capital and showplace of Russia came to an abrupt end.

Peter detested Moscow and the Kremlin, and with good reason. Born in 1672, Peter spent his early years in a court filled with suspicion, intrigue, and murder. Proclaimed czar at the age of ten, Peter experienced a horrifying incident that colored his feelings about the Kremlin for the rest of his life.

His mother, the second wife of Alexis I, did not get along with the Miloslavskys, the family of her husband's first wife. Fearful of losing their

Peter the Great grew to shun Moscow and the Kremlin because of his early years spent in a court of intrigue and murder.

power and prestige to the new czarina, the Miloslavskys did their best to stir up hostilities toward Peter and his mother after Alexis died in 1676. Following Alexis's death, his half-brother Fyodor III ascended the throne, but Fyodor also died shortly thereafter. Alexis's other half-brother, Ivan, was next in line. Ivan, though, was mentally incompetent and could not assume the throne, a problem that created a crisis within the monarchy. In 1682, the Miloslavskys saw their chance to do away with Peter and his mother, and they used this royal crisis to stir up the *strelsky*, an elite corps of soldiers who served the royal family. Spreading rumors that Peter would not listen to the grievances of the *strelsky*, the Miloslavskys encouraged the soldiers to take to the streets in protest.

The *strelsky* roamed the Kremlin for three days, destroying property and killing people. Even when Peter's mother appeared in public to reassure them and ask them to stop, the soldiers refused to end their rebellion. In fact, they stepped up their campaign of violence, killing several members of Peter's family. In the end, Peter and his mother fled the Kremlin. For the next seven years, they waited for an opportunity to return. Finally, in 1689, in a bloodless coup, Peter and his mother seized control of the throne, though Peter would not actually assume full control until 1694.

THE RED STAIRWAY

Running along the side of the Palace of the Facets is the Krasnoe Kryl'tso, the "Red Stairway" or "Beautiful Entrance." Decorated with painted and gilt lions, the sixteen-foot-wide stairway was covered with red carpets and was used as a ceremonial entrance when royalty visited the Kremlin.

The stairway has also been the scene of violence and bloodshed. Here, young Peter the Great witnessed the death of his mother's uncle at the hands of the crowd gathered around the stairs. His uncle was thrown from a palace window and landed on the pikes of the angry mob below. Seven years later, Peter stood atop the Red Stairway as the new czar of Russia.

The Kremlin's arsenal was constructed after the fire of 1701 to store military munitions and equipment, and artifacts and weaponry from defeated enemies.

To escape those bitter memories, Peter sought to build a brand-new capital city. Beginning in 1703 and continuing for the next twenty years, Peter's energies were consumed with the building of St. Petersburg. Because Peter ordered all available stonemasons to work at the new capital, the Kremlin and its buildings fell into disuse and decline until almost the middle of the eighteenth century. On the rare occasions when repairs were made to the aging fortress, they were often deficient, temporary, and incomplete. Meanwhile, the Kremlin's old foe, fire, continued periodically to ravage the complex.

THE ARSENAL

Peter did, however, construct one new building at the Kremlin, the arsenal. Built after Moscow's great fire of 1701, the arsenal was intended not only to store military munitions and equipment but also artifacts and weaponry from defeated enemies of Russia. In fact, Peter ordered all armament and insignia captured during battle to be brought to the arsenal, where they would be used as a war memorial commemorating Russian military victories. The construction of the arsenal dragged on for several years and was not completed until 1736. When finished, the building stood two stories high and was constructed of white stone.

A RUSSIAN VERSAILLES

The fortunes of the Kremlin appeared to take a turn for the better when Catherine II, known as Catherine the Great, assumed the throne in 1762. Although Catherine harbored no great love

Catherine the Great envisioned a Kremlin that would match the glory of Versailles.

for the Kremlin, having often complained of the dark and drafty royal residences located there, she recognized its importance and the need for more serious repairs and renovations if it were going to survive. She also envisioned the rebuilding effort as a means of transforming the Kremlin into the Russian equivalent of Versailles, the great French palace built by King Louis XIV.

Enlisting the help of Russian architect Vasilli Bazhenov, Catherine set out to reconstruct the Kremlin. She ordered the ground cleared and instructed Bazhenov to draw up blueprints. For months, he labored over these drawings. An architectural historian describes the large wooden model, which was four years in the making and depicted the new design of the Kremlin:

> The plan was to unite the whole Kremlin, having a circumference [boundary] of two miles, into one magnificent palace. . . . Triangular [in] form . . . every part of it [the model] was finished in the most beautiful manner, even to the fresco painting on the ceilings of the rooms, and the coloring of the various marble columns intended to decorate the interior.[20]

Work on the new project began in earnest in 1769. To make the design work, though, several buildings needed to be removed. These included the fifteenth-century treasury building, some administrative buildings, a few churches, three towers, and a section of the Kremlin wall. Four years later, on June 1, 1773, Catherine attended a glittering ceremony to mark the formal laying of the cornerstone for her Kremlin.

Soon, however, she lost interest in the project and, in time, completely abandoned her plans for the new construction. Her official reason was that the soil of the Kremlin could not possibly support the massive new structures that Bazhenov wanted to build. Unofficially, though, many people believe the reason was that Catherine had decided to pursue military conquests for Russia instead. Despite his pleas, Bazhenov could not persuade Catherine to change her mind. In the end, only the towers and the destroyed portion of the wall were ever rebuilt. All that remained of Catherine's Russian Versailles was the massive wooden model showing the projected new Kremlin.

OTHER BUILDING PROJECTS

Although Catherine the Great lost interest in rebuilding the Kremlin, she did recognize the need to do something about its sad state of disrepair. She went to Matvei Kazakov, a coworker of Bazhenov, to plan a number of new buildings. She then decided that Kazakov could build two of the buildings he had proposed. The first, completed in 1775, was a residence for the archbishop, known as the Archbishop's House.

RUSSIAN ARCHITECTURE

With increased exposure to European influences, Russian architecture continued to blend native styles with Western elements to create a unique, ever-changing type of architecture. From the time of Ivan IV on, for example, Russian architecture was characterized by a wild array of styles, including symmetrical columns, polychrome surfaces, and masses of onion domes grouped together. During the eighteenth century, though, Russian architecture changed to reflect some of the current trends in the West. These included incorporating oval spaces, curved surfaces, ornate decoration, and vivid color. Under Catherine the Great, the national architecture changed yet again, reflecting the quiet simplicity of the neoclassical style in imitation of Greek, Roman, Renaissance, and French forms. Whatever style they borrowed, though, Russian architects remained keenly aware of their own architectural heritage and never completely surrendered their legacy to Western tastes.

The following year ground was broken for a second building, one to house the Russian senate. Completed in 1787, the
senate building is located at the northeast corner of the Kremlin.
The building, constructed of white stone, is still considered one
of the best examples of Russian classical architecture, a style
that is simple in plan and is accented with classical forms such
as columns. The overall shape of the senate building is that of a
blunt-ended triangle. Arranged around the central, circular St.
Catherine Hall are eighteen columns that are eighty feet in diameter and ninety feet high. Between them are symbolic figures
depicting such virtues as justice and philanthropy. There are
also a number of carvings depicting events from Catherine's
reign. With the completion of the senate building and the Archbishop's House, all construction in the Kremlin ended for the
next fifty years.

DESTRUCTION AND RECONSTRUCTION

During this fifty-year period, the Kremlin housed invaders within
its walls for the second time in its history. On June 24, 1812,
French emperor Napoléon Bonaparte invaded Russia with an
army of 424,000 troops. Overwhelmed by the massive strength of

*Napoléon Bonaparte and his troops invaded Russia on June 24, 1812. One week later,
they entered the city of Moscow.*

Shortly after the city was taken by Napoléon and his troops, 80 percent of Moscow was destroyed by fires set by hidden arsonists.

Napoléon's army, the Russian troops retreated, drawing Napoléon after them in pursuit. By the time Napoléon entered Moscow one week later, on September 14, 1812, his army, reduced by casualties, illness, and desertions, numbered only 115,000 men.

Having taken Moscow, Napoléon expected Czar Alexander I to initiate negotiations for surrender, but he waited in vain. The Russians had virtually abandoned the city. "Moscow," wrote one French soldier, "seems to us to be a huge corpse. . . the kingdom of silence."[21] French soldiers began to loot the city, stealing the treasures that the Muscovites had left behind as they fled. When, toward nightfall, French sentries noticed wisps of smoke rising, they attributed them to accidental fires started by the disorderly troops. Napoléon had already gone to bed before the lookouts realized how wrong they had been.

By the time one of Napoléon's subordinates roused him from sleep, Moscow was engulfed in flames. The apparently empty city actually concealed hundreds of arsonists, who set fires everywhere. Before rain put out the fires, 80 percent of Moscow, including much of Red Square, was in ashes, although the Kremlin itself was barely touched.

What fire did not destroy, the French troops did. The soldiers, confined to tents pitched in the Kremlin squares or in other buildings of the fort, showed little interest in or respect for the old fortress, its buildings, or its treasures. They removed furniture and used it for kindling. The rations and equipment of Napoléon's cavalry were kept in one of the Kremlin's many churches. Next to revered relics of Russian saints in the Church of the Assumption, the French erected a furnace to melt down stolen gold and silver candlesticks, plates, and jewelry. Worse, the cavalry stabled its horses in St. Basil's cathedral.

When Alexander I refused to surrender, Napoléon decided to abandon Moscow and ordered that the Kremlin be destroyed. To that end, one of his generals had 183,000 pounds of gunpowder placed under the walls of the fortress as well as in other buildings throughout the compound. When the retreating French touched off the powder, it produced a terrible explosion.

Although the damage was great, much of the old fortress, now more than five centuries old, withstood the blast. However, the explosion did destroy the royal residence and a section of the arsenal. It badly damaged two gates and the Ivan the Great Bell Tower. In some spots, the explosion even opened huge holes in walls.

Gradually, though, order returned, and Czar Alexander's first order of business was rebuilding the Kremlin. In 1814 he appointed architect Osip Ivanovich Beauvais chairman of a special commission for reconstruction. Beauvais began his work by clearing away the wreckage in Red Square and by redesigning the square to emphasize the historical connection between it and the Kremlin.

Beauvais went on to complete many other projects. Repairs and reconstruction work were carried out on the Terem Palace and the arsenal. The walls and streets throughout the Kremlin were repaired or replaced. The Ivan the Great Bell Tower was also repaired, though the structure would never again stand completely straight.

EASTERN AND WESTERN INFLUENCES

By the mid–nineteenth century Russia was enjoying a relative period of peace, and the new czar, Nicholas I, contemplated building a grand new structure that would house the royal family. More than a royal residence, this structure would become a symbol of the growing tension between Western influence and Russian tradition. Nicholas I was a passionate nationalist and thus promoted Russian art and culture. He and his supporters viewed Western ways as decadent and threatening to Russian life. If Western influences were allowed to flourish as they had under Peter the Great and Catherine, the nationalists believed, they would ultimately stifle Russia's own vibrant traditions.

This cultural struggle played itself out in architecture with the construction of the Great Kremlin Palace, the last great structure built at the Kremlin during the nineteenth century. Situated along the south side of Kremlin Hill, the palace, which contains more than seven hundred rooms, was built between 1838 and 1849 by Konstantin A. Ton, the leading Russian architect of the period. The czar, in granting this prestigious

Czar Nicholas I denounced Western art as decadent and instead promoted Russian art and culture.

commission to Ton, clearly spelled out his desire for a building that symbolized the Russian spirit in architecture.

THE GREAT KREMLIN PALACE

In fact, a new palace was long overdue. The rooms at the Terem Palace were small and lacked modern amenities. They were also on the shabby side and had become a source of embarrassment for the royal family. Then, too, there was the general run-down appearance of the Kremlin, which did not make a favorable impression on foreign visitors. It was clear that something needed to be done.

Nicholas envisioned the Great Kremlin Palace as a remedy for this situation. When completed, the palace would cover over five hundred thousand square feet and include within it the Palace of the Facets, the Church of the Holy Vestibule, the czarina's Golden Chamber, the Terem Palace, and other palace cathedrals and churches.

In building the new quarters, Ton demolished several old structures and incorporated the existing royal residences and churches into one large, interconnected group of buildings. The

Dissatisfied with the condition of the Terem Palace, Nicholas I commissioned the Great Kremlin Palace, a building that would incorporate many of the Kremlin's royal residences and churches.

quadrangular palace covers a large portion of Kremlin Hill, and its gilt, dome-shaped pavilion is visible for miles. The brightly painted yellow-stone building stands two stories high. The first floor of the palace has two tiers of windows; the second floor, one tier. White-stone carvings are found throughout the building on the window frames, the walls, and the roof.

The main wing of the palace is magnificent. It includes a granite staircase that ascends five flights and interior rooms that are graced with stuccoed decorations, rare woods, unique marble and alabaster columns, crystal chandeliers, and gold. Furthermore, every hallway is adorned with the colors of the different royal families.

The palace is also composed of many halls, the largest of which is the Hall of St. George. Measuring two hundred feet long, sixty-eight feet wide, and fifty-eight feet high, the hall was named after the highest military honor given by the Russians, the St. George Cross. Six gilt chandeliers, each weighing more than two tons, light the hall, and along the walls are niches filled with marble slabs. On each slab, inscribed in gold, are the names of the various regiments in the Russian army as well as the names of individuals who distinguished themselves in battle.

The private apartments of the royal family, located on the ground floor, included seven rooms: a dining room, the empress's drawing or reception room, the empress's study and dressing room, the bedroom, the emperor's study and reception room, and four additional rooms in which courtiers and servants stayed. Each room was furnished with a special set of furniture and art objects, including priceless porcelain, crystal, jewels, and bronzes. Today, the rooms are used for receptions to honor foreign dignitaries.

The reign of the Romanovs, although mostly unspectacular, was important because it was an era during which the royal family was devoted to maintaining and improving the Kremlin and its buildings. The monarchy also allowed more people to come and visit the Kremlin during this time. In the waning years of czarist Russia and Romanov rule, the Kremlin was open to all who wished to visit.

White-stone carvings decorate the window frames of the Great Kremlin Palace.

Russians and foreigners alike came through the gates to marvel at the majestic buildings. On any Sunday afternoon in good weather, people walked through the parklike grounds and children played among the monuments and statues. The Kremlin might have continued in its role as an aging museum of Russian history, but other, more calamitous events were already beginning to unfold.

THE CENTER OF
THE SOVIET STATE

The Russian Empire was vast. It stretched from Germany to Japan, covering one-sixth of the land surface of the earth. Yet the Russian Empire also suffered from severe problems, most of which proved to be insurmountable. The sheer size of the empire, the adverse climate, the poor communications, and the extensive ethnic, cultural, linguistic, and religious diversity made Russia a backward country compared to its western European neighbors.

The Russian Empire had been created by conquest and was held together by force. Its rulers lived in permanent fear of foreign invasion and internal revolution. Throughout the nineteenth and early twentieth centuries, the future of Russia depended on whether the government could maintain political order.

THE TRAGEDY OF CZARIST RUSSIA

Of all of the countries in nineteenth-century Europe, Russia remained the most authoritarian and autocratic. The spectacle of dissident political parties, social unrest, and periodic revolution in western European countries such as France reinforced to Russian rulers the necessity of maintaining a strong, authoritarian government. The Russian ruling elite, along with a large segment of the educated public, feared that the peasants, who constituted 90 percent of the country's population, would go on a rampage if they sensed a weakening of authority.

Despite various political and social reforms carried out during the second half of the nineteenth century, Russia, by the early twentieth century, was still a weak and backward country. Between 1825 and 1914 the rulers of Russia labored under enormous disabilities to equal and, if possible, to exceed the power and prestige of the great states of western Europe. They failed, and the public's resentment of the government grew.

THE LAST CZAR

Czar Nicholas II came to the Russian imperial throne in 1894, following the death of his father, Alexander III. Nicholas was woefully unprepared to assume the responsibilities of power. He was better suited in temperament to the life of a country squire than to his role as czar of Russia. He was more interested in his family than in the government, and so he spent most of his time trying to resist the demands for reform that came from various elements within the empire.

The nobility, the military, the workers, the middle class, and the peasants all wanted certain changes to be made in Russian government and society, although they rarely agreed on what changes ought to be implemented and for whose benefit. Czar Nicholas tried his best to defy them all by simply ignoring the problems and thus preserving the dynasty he had inherited.

THE COMING OF REVOLUTION

Although the Russian people, like their counterparts throughout Europe, had responded with patriotic fervor to the outbreak of World War I in 1914, by 1916 they were in despair. The Russian army, for the most part ill equipped, poorly led, and suffering incredible losses, was disintegrating. At home, shops were empty, money was worthless, and the population was cold and starving. Strikes and

Czar Nicholas II displayed more interest in his family than in his people's demands for reform.

riots ravaged Russian cities. Still, Nicholas II, determined to preserve his autocratic rule, refused to consider making reforms to ease the burdens on his people and to aid the Russian war effort.

Fear of revolution had long troubled foresighted Russians. In 1917 these long-standing fears became a reality. On March 8, 1917, the citizens of Petrograd (formerly St. Petersburg) rose up demanding food. Their protest quickly escalated out of control. Angry crowds demonstrated in the streets during the days that followed. The army, which had stood by the czar earlier, abandoned

Russian soldiers aiding the Petrograd demonstrators prepare to defend themselves against any comrades who remained loyal to Czar Nicholas II.

him when, on March 10, the soldiers, ordered to disperse the mob, instead turned their guns on the police and rushed to support the demonstrators. The Romanov dynasty, which had ruled Russia for more than three hundred years, was about to end.

Having lost control of the army, Czar Nicholas II faced the inevitable; on March 15, 1917, he abdicated the throne in his own name and that of his son, Alexis. He turned power over to his brother, Grand Duke Michael. The following day, March 16, 1917, Michael also abdicated the crown.

In the week before the czar abdicated, two rival centers of power had emerged in Petrograd. First, there was the Petrograd Soviet, a council representing the protesters and the soldiers who aided them. Second, there was a committee of liberals, many of whom had been members of the imperial Duma, the Russian legislature. Although these men wished to be rid of the czar, they hated and feared revolution and the Petrograd Soviet. The liberals moved to establish a governmental body called the Provisional Government under the leadership of Prince Georgy Lvov.

RED OCTOBER

In October 1917 Red Square and the Kremlin again became the scene of bitter fighting, this time not between Russians and

Tatars but between the adherents of the liberal Provisional Government and those of the revolutionary Soviets. In the ensuing struggle between the supporters of the Provisional Government and the Soviets, the Kremlin and Red Square were the targets of machine guns, mortars, and artillery that did considerable damage to the Kremlin walls, towers, and cathedrals as well as to the other buildings located in Red Square.

"They are bombarding the Kremlin!" wrote American journalist John Reed, who witnessed the October Revolution. He and the Russians themselves were shocked that their own countrymen were destroying the most sacred of Russian historical monuments. Reed later wrote, "Nothing that the Bolsheviki [Soviets] had done could compare with this fearful blasphemy in the heart of Holy Russia. To the ears of the devout sounded the shock of guns crashing in the face of the Holy Orthodox Church, and pounding to dust the sanctuary of the Russian nation."[22]

The damage done to the Kremlin was considerable. The Soviets bombarded and plundered Nikolai Palace, near the Saviour's Gate. They also partially destroyed the Beklemishev Tower. A shell pierced one of the cupolas of the Cathedral of the Assumption, and gunfire scarred the frescoes of the Cathedral of the Annunciation. Shells also riddled the Ivan the Great Bell

The Nikolai Palace (pictured) and many other structures in the Kremlin were damaged during the October 1917 revolution.

Tower and the Chudov Monastery, destroyed the clock and chimes of the Saviour's Tower, and battered the Trinity Gate. Fortunately, no harm came to the Cathedral of St. Basil or the Great Kremlin Palace.

One element of the Kremlin that did not survive the fighting was the icon of St. Nicholas that hung over the St. Nicholas Gate, one of the five entrance gates to the Kremlin. The icon, thought to be indestructible, was shot full of holes and was destroyed. Through the centuries, the icon had remained unharmed by fire, invaders, and inclement weather. Even after Napoléon's attempt to blow up the Kremlin, the icon remained in place. Now, like so many other Russian treasures, it, too, was gone.

THE COMMUNIST KREMLIN

Almost overnight the Kremlin underwent a remarkable transformation. No longer considered an aging historical museum, when the Communists seized power in 1917 the fortress was deemed the new home of the Soviet government. For the first time since Peter the Great had moved the capital to St. Petersburg, the Kremlin was once more the literal and symbolic center of the nation's power. In March 1918 the capital was formally transferred back to Moscow, with the most important government and Communist, or Soviet, Party offices headquartered in the Kremlin.

Like the earlier rulers of Russia, the new Communist leaders lived in the Kremlin. Unlike the czars, who savored the lavish

THE GRANITE OBELISK TO REVOLUTIONARY AND SOCIALIST THINKERS

In 1918 a light-colored granite obelisk, a four-sided stone monument, measuring a little more than sixty-five feet high, was constructed not far from the Corner Arsenal Tower. This monument is known as the Granite Obelisk to Revolutionary and Socialist Thinkers. Carved on one side of the memorial are the names of those people who helped promote the ideals of socialism, including Karl Marx, Friedrich Engels, and a number of Russian intellectuals and socialist thinkers. In 1967 the obelisk was moved closer to the Middle Arsenal Tower, helping to create a special memorial section at the Kremlin wall.

and opulent surroundings, the new government officials, at least in the early days of Communist rule, stressed simplicity and austerity, which was more in keeping with the Communist philosophy. As a result, the nation's new leaders lived in spartan conditions, often residing in small, sparsely furnished apartments that had been converted from offices in administration buildings, and taking their meals in a communal dining hall that accommodated three hundred people. In the senate building, where the boyars had once advised the czars, the Central Committee of the Communist Party now convened. Following the death of Yakov Sverdlov, the first president of the Soviet Union, in 1919, the hall was renamed Sverdlov Hall in his honor.

Despite the Soviet leaders' claim that theirs was a government of and for the people, the new administration did all it could to discourage visitors from entering the Kremlin. They ordered the fortress sealed off from the rest of Moscow and posted guards at the gates to stop unwanted visitors from entering. The secrecy was so intense that even foreign dignitaries were forbidden to enter the Kremlin, often having to settle for meetings with Soviet officials outside the fortress walls.

REPAIRING THE KREMLIN

During the early years of Soviet rule, the emphasis was on maintaining power and stabilizing the country. This meant that badly needed repair work for the Kremlin was left undone. In 1920, though, the Soviet government slowly began a program of restoration and reconstruction at the Kremlin. A special restoration commission, composed of architects, archaeologists, and painters, supervised the repair of the walls, towers, and churches of the Kremlin and of Red Square. The commission also undid many of the numerous alterations, such as the whitewashed brick walls that had been added over the years. Further, the government also began extensive repair and reconstruction work on several of the Kremlin's buildings, during which laborers discovered old artwork, icons, and forgotten passageways. The goal of the commission was to restore the Kremlin to the splendor it had enjoyed during the reigns of Ivan III and Ivan IV.

LENIN IN THE KREMLIN

Vladimir Ilich Ulyanov, who went by the name of Lenin, was one of the main forces behind the Bolshevik revolution and was the first premier of the Soviet Union. Lenin lived and worked in the Kremlin for five years, from 1918 until 1923, when declining health forced him to leave public life.

The Soviet government occupied the senate building, and it was here that Lenin set up his study—a small, modestly furnished room with a high vaulted ceiling. Equally spartan was the first apartment that Lenin and his wife, Nadezhda Krupskaya, occupied in the Kremlin: just two small rooms in the Chevalier Guards building. After completion of repairs to the court offices, Lenin, his wife, and his sister, Maria Ulyanova, settled into a four-room apartment on the offices' second floor. Lenin's wife and sister lived in this apartment the remainder of their lives, preserving the furnishings and the interior exactly as they had been in Lenin's day.

Above: Vladimir Lenin works at a desk at the Kremlin. Below: The Lenin Mausoleum, built to house Lenin's embalmed remains.

The Presidium, or president's residence, was constructed between 1932 and 1934 under the direction of Joseph Stalin.

When Lenin died in 1924, the government constructed the Lenin Mausoleum, built to house Lenin's embalmed remains and to commemorate the Russian Revolution. Originally built of wood until a permanent structure could be completed, the Lenin Mausoleum was to be the new focal point of Red Square. The base of the mausoleum is elevated slightly above the level of the square and is enclosed by a low parapet, or wall. The monument is constructed of different types of stone and stands stern, powerful, and austere, suggestive of both the character of the man it commemorates and the ideals of the Bolshevik revolution.

THE BUILDING OF THE PRESIDIUM

Succeeding Lenin was Iosif Vissarionovich Dzhugashvili, who went by the name of Joseph Stalin. Under Stalin's direction, the Communists undertook additional construction projects in the Kremlin. Located not far from the Saviour's Gate, for instance, was one of the largest projects built, the Presidium, or the president's residence. Designed by a Russian architect and constructed between 1932 and 1934, the three-story white-stone building also housed government offices. In style, color, and proportions, the Presidium complemented the older senate building, built during the reign of Catherine the Great and located close by.

TO FINLAND STATION

By 1900 a number of young, educated Russians had rallied to the revolutionary teachings of the German thinker Karl Marx, who believed that the downtrodden masses would one day rise up against those who trapped them in poverty and misery. The most articulate of these young, revolutionary

Russian revolutionary Vladimir Lenin gives a speech before a crowd in Moscow in 1919.

The government put the Presidium to many uses. At first, the building accommodated a military school. Then, in 1938, it was converted into a government meeting hall. The Soviet government, which consisted of the two chambers called the Soviet of Nationalities and the Council of Elders, convened in the Presidium to debate and manage affairs of state.

WELCOMING VISITORS AGAIN

During Stalin's regime, the Kremlin was also opened on a limited basis to the public. Beginning in the 1930s, both Russians and foreign visitors were allowed to visit Kremlin museums and palaces. Foreign dignitaries were also formally received within the Kremlin walls; on occasion, special social functions were

Russian Marxists was Vladimir Lenin. Born in the provincial Russian town of Simbirsk, Lenin was the son of a teacher and a school administrator. He studied law at the University of Kazan and received his law degree from the University of St. Petersburg in 1891.

While a law student in St. Petersburg, Lenin joined an illegal circle of Social Democratic propagandists. His opinions and activities cost him three years (1897–1900) in Siberia. Afterward, he left Russia and took up residence briefly in Germany and then in Switzerland. Living in Switzerland, Lenin, his wife, and a small group of followers planned to seize power in Russia should an opportunity ever present itself.

When Czar Nicholas II abdicated and the new provisional government announced its intention to keep Russia fighting against Germany in World War I, the Germans hoped that Lenin could disrupt this effort. German agents made discreet inquiries and found Lenin receptive to accepting German money and German assistance in exchange for his attempt to seize control of Russia. The Germans enabled Lenin to return from exile, providing him and his companions with a sealed train that carried them from Switzerland across Germany and Sweden, and then on to Finland Station, the first railroad stop inside Russia.

held in the former receiving and reception rooms of the royal residences. But only a decade after the Soviets opened them, the Kremlin gates were shut once more, as Stalin began his infamous purges in which hundreds of thousands of Russians lost their lives. Stalin himself rarely left the Kremlin.

THE MOST WELL-KEPT SPOT IN THE SOVIET UNION

Throughout Stalin's rule, the Soviet government did its best to keep the Kremlin in good condition, with no trace of the shabbiness or run-down appearance that had once characterized it. An American writer visiting the Kremlin in 1949 described its condition: "The various buildings and grounds inside the Kremlin are as neat and polished as the tiled bathroom fixtures, the only

PRESERVING A LEGACY

The Soviets may have overthrown the czarist regime, but they took great care in preserving the czar's palaces and belongings. Even today, tourists who visit the royal palaces in the Kremlin see rooms with the czar's furnishings intact. Dining room tables are set with ornate silver and gold dishes and silverware; bedchambers display expensive silk coverlets and heavy silk and velvet curtains. Museum guides in the palaces even wear soft felt slippers to make sure that the expensive wooden floors maintain their original condition.

The purpose of this extreme care and attention was twofold. First, the Communists used the lavish displays of royal wealth as means of teaching a lesson about how the wealthy lived at the expense of the poor. More important, though, the Communist government took seriously its responsibility as caretaker of Russian historical treasures and, to that end, tried to preserve them for the people of Russia.

Tourists can still witness the well-preserved rooms and furnishings of the Kremlin's palaces.

really well-kept spot I've seen in the Soviet Union. Even the blades of grass looked as though they had been straightened that morning."[23] Another visitor noted that the Kremlin was "an expanse of broad well-kept lawns, prim borders planted with young shrubs, and official looking stuccoed buildings with wide windows."[24] In addition to keeping the grounds and buildings in good condition, Stalin's government systematically and carefully cataloged all of the valuable Kremlin artifacts.

The Soviets also made changes in the Kremlin that reflected their government. They removed the old imperial coat of arms that decorated the tower spires and replaced them with red Soviet stars. They also did away with other symbols of the czarist government, such as the double-headed Byzantine eagle, and put up in their place portraits of Communist leaders and emblems depicting the hammer and sickle or sheaves of wheat, symbols of the international Communist movement.

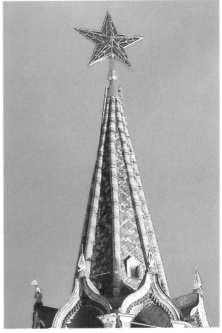

Russia's Communist government replaced the imperial coats of arms that used to cap the pinnacles of the Kremlin's towers with red stars.

And Stalin realized that the buildings themselves needed to be updated and modernized. Over time, the Kremlin's buildings were equipped to handle electricity, modern plumbing, heating and air conditioning, telephones, and other communication devices.

The early years of the twentieth century brought a new form of government to Russia, one that took seriously its responsibility as a caretaker for one of the nation's oldest buildings. Not only did the Communist government give the Kremlin a new identity, but it also salvaged and repaired earlier damage and destruction that threatened the compound's existence.

Epilogue

On March 3, 1953, the body of Communist leader Joseph Stalin was placed next to that of Vladimir Lenin. Stalin's death signaled a new direction in the policies of the Soviet government as well as some important changes for the Kremlin. During the next thirty-eight years, the Kremlin would adapt as conditions in the Soviet Union changed.

A New Beginning

Although new construction began tapering off at the beginning of the twentieth century, by the 1950s reconstruction and new construction were underway at the Kremlin. The Kremlin Theater opened at the Presidium in 1958, showcasing dance, theater, and musical events. And at the end of 1959, the Winter Garden was completed and opened in the Great Kremlin Palace.

Located on the first floor, this indoor garden was designed to resemble the old seventeenth-century gardens that had once graced the palace. It covers approximately thirty-four hundred square feet, with almost twelve hundred square feet devoted to the more than seventeen hundred tropical and subtropical plants that grow there. The garden's west wall is enclosed completely by glass to provide sunlight for the plants and flowers. The east wall is made of mirrors that reflect the groups of plants and flow-

The Palace of Congresses, also known as the White House, is a glass and marble building that contains some eight hundred offices.

ers growing throughout. On the south wall is a niche decorated with colored and gilded mosaic enamel. Nearby lies a goldfish pond in which a small hill made of colored pieces of crystal rises from the center into a miniature fountain lit from underneath.

The south and north walls are made of marble, and the floor is covered with a special stone cut from the quarries of Armenia.

In addition, the government proceeded with plans to build a contemporary government building, the Palace of Congresses, also known as the White House. Built in a little more than two years, this palace formally opened its doors on October 17, 1961, in time to commemorate the forty-fourth anniversary of the October Revolution. The building is constructed of glass and marble and contains some eight hundred offices and a main hall that seats six thousand people.

During the days of the Soviet Union, the Palace of Congresses was used to hold the sessions of the Communist Party, international Communist congresses, meetings, and conferences of all types. The building was also used for public performances of the ballet and opera, major celebrations, New Year's fes-

Russian president Vladimir Putin attends his May 2000 inauguration ceremony at the Kremlin.

tivities, and other ceremonial state functions. The five-story building is rectangular, measuring 397 feet long, almost 240 feet wide, and 89 feet high, and the interior covers more than 523,000 square yards, with a total floor area of 72,700 square yards.

THE KREMLIN TODAY

Since the collapse of the Soviet Union in 1991, though, the Kremlin has undergone even more changes. For example, the Great Kremlin Palace is now the scene of presidential inaugurations as Russia struggles to move from a socialist to a democratic republic. Further, in November 1992 "God officially returned to the Kremlin,"[25] announced one magazine, as the Russian state handed back control of the cathedrals to the Russian Orthodox Church, which had been silenced for more than seventy-five years under the Communist regime.

The secular culture of the Kremlin changed with the restructuring of Russian society as well. During the last decades of the twentieth century, the Kremlin, once the scene of so many invasions, provided the setting for an invasion of another kind: that of rock-and-roll groups. Popular bands from the United States and Europe have performed to enthusiastic crowds, anxious to hear Western pop music.

Despite the renovations and additions, though, the Kremlin, in keeping with its long and often troubled past, is once again in danger. Even though the Russian government has rebuilt some of the older churches demolished during and after the Bolshevik revolution, the majority of the Kremlin is in poor condition. Portions of the buildings are beginning to crumble. Bricks are falling from the towers. Roofs, such as the one on the armory, are leaking badly. Additionally, the churches all need cleaning and a coat of paint.

The last refurbishing of the Kremlin was done in the 1980s. Since then, the Russian government has earmarked about

ARCHAEOLOGICAL DISCOVERIES

In the last few years, archaeological investigations have been uncovering exciting new evidence of the Kremlin's ancient past. In the 1980s and 1990s, Russian archaeologists began conducting extensive excavations in and around Moscow. Digging in the area of the northeastern section of the Kremlin in 1988 and 1991 uncovered hoards of silver jewelry thought to date from the twelfth and thirteenth centuries. Archaeologists speculated that the find may have been treasure buried around the time of the Tatar invasions of Batu Khan. Excavations around Red Square also uncovered a variety of interesting artifacts, such as the remains of earlier churches and residue from the fire of 1493. An early birch-bark document was also uncovered, the only one of its kind ever found in Moscow.

$4.9 million to restore the Kremlin and its buildings. But because of the deteriorating financial condition of the country as well as political turmoil, the money has yet to be given to the Kremlin's administrators. Although many people fear that this may prove to be a sad ending for the place where Moscow began, others recognize that the Kremlin has been in jeopardy many times before and has always survived.

RUSSIA'S GREATEST TREASURE

Nowhere else in the world is there a place like the Kremlin. During its long history, it has been transformed from the center of a small, struggling town to the center of an expanding kingdom to the center of a vast empire. Despite the many foreign influences, both welcome and unwelcome, that have shaped its history, the Kremlin has always remained unmistakably Russian. Yet the appeal and importance of the Kremlin extend beyond Russia. Although its buildings illustrate the emergence of a Russian architectural style, they also merge the vibrant and sometimes whimsical Russian imagination with the elaborate and opulent art of the Byzantine world and the elegant, graceful, and dignified vision of the Italian

The Kremlin showcases a blend of architectural influences yet remains unmistakably Russian.

Renaissance. Taken together, this combination of elements and viewpoints makes for a unique group of buildings, the likes of which the world has no equal.

From its inception, the Kremlin has united the secular and spiritual history and heritage of Russia. In the end, perhaps only the folk wisdom and memory contained in a Russian proverb can capture and convey the meaning that the Kremlin has had for the Russian people: "There is nothing above Moscow except the Kremlin, and nothing above the Kremlin except Heaven."[26]

NOTES

Introduction

1. Arthur Voyce, *The Moscow Kremlin: Its History, Architecture, and Art Treasures.* Berkeley and Los Angeles: University of California Press, 1954, p. 3.

Chapter 1: A Citadel of Wood

2. Quoted in Abraham Ascher, *The Kremlin.* New York: Newsweek Books, 1978, p. 14.
3. Quoted in Irina Rodimtseva, *The Moscow Kremlin: A Guide.* Leningrad, Russia: Aurora Art, 1987, p. 10.
4. Quoted in Victor Alexandrov, *The Kremlin: Nerve-Centre of Russian History.* New York: St. Martin's, 1963, p. 30.
5. Quoted in Alexandrov, *The Kremlin*, p. 30.

Chapter 2: From Wood to Stone

6. Quoted in Ascher, *The Kremlin*, p. 20.

Chapter 3: Unmistakably Russian

7. Quoted in Jules Koslow, *The Kremlin: Eight Centuries of Tyranny and Terror.* New York: Thomas Nelson & Sons, 1958, p. 28.
8. Quoted in George Heard Hamilton, *The Art and Architecture of Russia.* New Haven, CT: Yale University Press, 1983, p. 232.
9. Arthur Voyce, *The Art and Architecture of Medieval Russia.* Norman: University of Oklahoma Press, 1967, p. 153.
10. William Craft Brumfield, *Gold in Azure: One Thousand Years of Russian Architecture.* New York: David R. Godine, 1983, p. 141.
11. Quoted in Voyce, *The Art and Architecture of Medieval Russia*, p. 157.
12. Quoted in Susan Massie, *Land of the Firebird.* New York: Simon & Schuster, 1980, p. 46.
13. Voyce, *The Moscow Kremlin*, p. 25.
14. Voyce, *The Moscow Kremlin*, p. 46.

Chapter 4: The Kremlin in Turmoil

15. Quoted in Voyce, *The Moscow Kremlin*, p. 23.

16. Koslow, *The Kremlin*, p. 73.

17. Quoted in Voyce, *The Moscow Kremlin*, p. 95.

18. Voyce, *The Moscow Kremlin*, p. 96.

Chapter 5: Abandoned and Rescued

19. Quoted in Hamilton, *The Art and Architecture of Russia*, p. 233.

20. Voyce, *The Moscow Kremlin*, p. 62.

21. Quoted in Editors of Time-Life Books, *What Life Was Like in the Time of War and Peace: Imperial Russia, A.D. 1696–1917.* Alexandria, VA: Time-Life Books, 1998, p. 53.

Chapter 6: The Center of the Soviet State

22. Quoted in Koslow, *The Kremlin*, p. 216.

23. Quoted in Koslow, *The Kremlin*, p. 228.

24. Quoted in Koslow, *The Kremlin*, p. 228.

Epilogue

25. *World & I,* "God Returns to Kremlin," February, 1993, p. 135.

26. Quoted in Editors of Time-Life Books, *What Life Was Like in the Time of War and Peace*, p. 20.

FOR FURTHER READING

Books

Abraham Ascher, *The Kremlin*. New York: Newsweek Books, 1978. An interesting historical overview of the Kremlin and its role in Russian history.

Laurel Corona, *Life in Moscow*. San Diego: Lucent Books, 2000. A detailed portrayal of life in modern-day Moscow.

David Douglas Duncan, *Great Treasures of the Kremlin*. New York: Harry N. Abrams, 1967. Beautiful images highlight this work on the Kremlin's art treasures.

Editors of Time-Life Books, *What Life Was Like in the Time of War and Peace: Imperial Russia, A.D. 1696–1917*. Alexandria, VA: Time-Life Books, 1998. A historical overview of late seventeenth- to early twentieth-century Russia.

Thomas Streissguth, *Life in Communist Russia*. San Diego: Lucent Books, 2000. An account of the way people lived during the seventy years following the establishment of the Soviet Union.

Arthur Voyce, *The Art and Architecture of Medieval Russia*. Norman: University of Oklahoma Press, 1967. A historic overview of the early history of the Kremlin and its architecture.

Website

The Moscow Kremlin (www.moscowkremlin.ru/NS/english/). The official site for the Kremlin; in Russian and English.

WORKS CONSULTED

Books

Victor Alexandrov, *The Kremlin: Nerve-Centre of Russian History*. New York: St. Martin's, 1963. A historical overview of the Kremlin.

William Craft Brumfield, *Gold in Azure: One Thousand Years of Russian Architecture*. New York: David R. Godine, 1983. A historical overview of Russian architecture, with special emphasis on the churches of the Kremlin.

George Heard Hamilton, *The Art and Architecture of Russia*. New Haven, CT: Yale University Press, 1983. Includes a good overview of the Kremlin's architectural history.

Jules Koslow, *The Kremlin: Eight Centuries of Tyranny and Terror*. New York: Thomas Nelson & Sons, 1958. A somewhat dated overview, but filled with good anecdotal and factual information about the Kremlin.

Susan Massie, *Land of the Firebird*. New York: Simon & Schuster, 1980. A cultural history of Russia, with some emphasis on the Kremlin and court life.

Bernard Meares, trans., *Around the Kremlin*. Moscow: Progress, 1967. An official guidebook and history of the Kremlin, with an emphasis on the Communist government's role in restoring the Kremlin, plus an excellent section on the Armory and its treasures.

Irina Rodimtseva, *The Kremlin: A Guide*. Leningrad, Russia: Aurora Art, 1987. The official guide book to the Kremlin.

Arthur Voyce, *The Moscow Kremlin: Its History, Architecture, and Art Treasures*. Berkeley and Los Angeles: University of California Press, 1954. One of the few books in English to focus specifically on the Kremlin and its buildings.

Periodical

World & I, "God Returns to Kremlin," February 1993.

INDEX

PICTURE CREDITS

ABOUT THE AUTHOR

Meg Greene is a writer and historian with a particular interest in architecture. She has a bachelor's degree in history from Lindenwood College, a master's degree in history from the University of Nebraska at Omaha, and a master's degree in historic preservation from the University of Vermont. She is the author of eight books, one of which—*Slave Young, Slave Long*—was recognized as a 1999 Honor Book by the Society of School Librarians International for grades seven through twelve. She is a regular contributor to *Cobblestone Magazine* and a contributing editor to "History for Children" for Suite 101.com. Ms. Greene makes her home in Virginia.